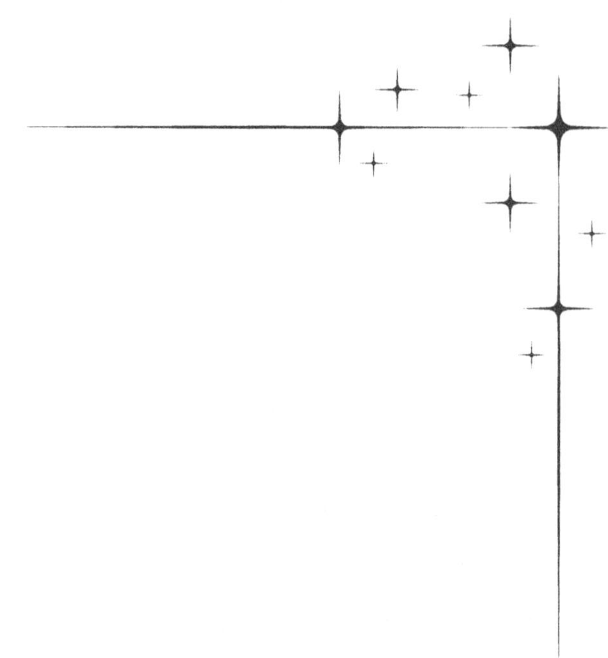

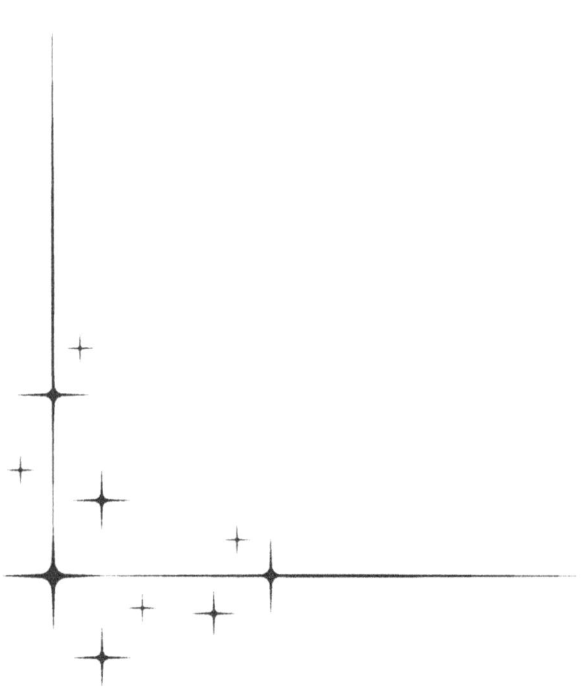

HELLO FRIEND,

THIS JOURNAL WAS MADE WITH LOVE FOR ALL WHO LIKE TO WRITE, JOURNAL, DOODLE, AND PRAY.

MY PRAYER JOURNAL IS MY MOST IMPORTANT BOOK, NEXT TO MY BIBLE. I HOPE THIS LITTLE BOOK WILL BLESS YOU AS MY PRAYER JOURNAL BLESSES ME.

YOUR FATHER IN HEAVEN WANTS TO HAVE A RELATIONSHIP WITH YOU. FIRST THESSALONIANS 5:16-18 SAYS: "REJOICE ALWAYS, PRAY WITHOUT CEASING, GIVE THANKS IN ALL CIRCUMSTANCES; FOR THIS IS THE WILL OF GOD IN CHRIST JESUS FOR YOU."

IN THE REVEALED BOOK SERIES, MADDIE CREATED A SIMPLE JOURNAL USING THE ACROSTIC- A.C.T.S.- TO INSPIRE YOU IN PRAYER. JUST WRITE, AND REMEMBER THAT YOUR HEAVENLY FATHER KNOWS YOUR HEART. THIS RHYTHM ALLOWS YOU TO RELEASE WHAT YOU ARE HOLDING INTO THE HANDS OF THE ONE WHO KNOWS JUST WHAT TO DO WITH IT.

SO GRAB YOUR BIBLE, AND LET'S TAKE A JOURNEY THROUGH PRAYER! WE ARE IN THE PRESENCE OF ALMIGHTY GOD!

MAY THE LORD BLESS YOU AND KEEP YOU. MAY HE MAKE HIS FACE TO SHINE UPON YOU AND BE GRACIOUS TO YOU. MAY HE TURN HIS FACE TO YOU AND GIVE YOU HIS PEACE (NUMBERS 6:24-26).

Eve

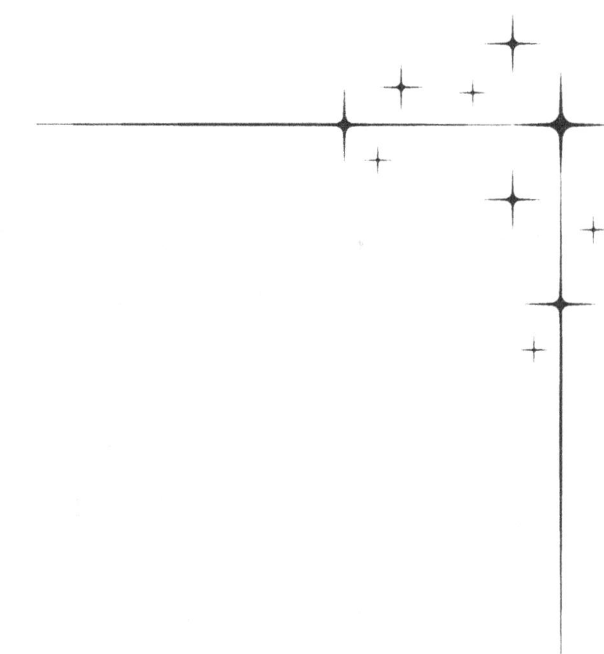

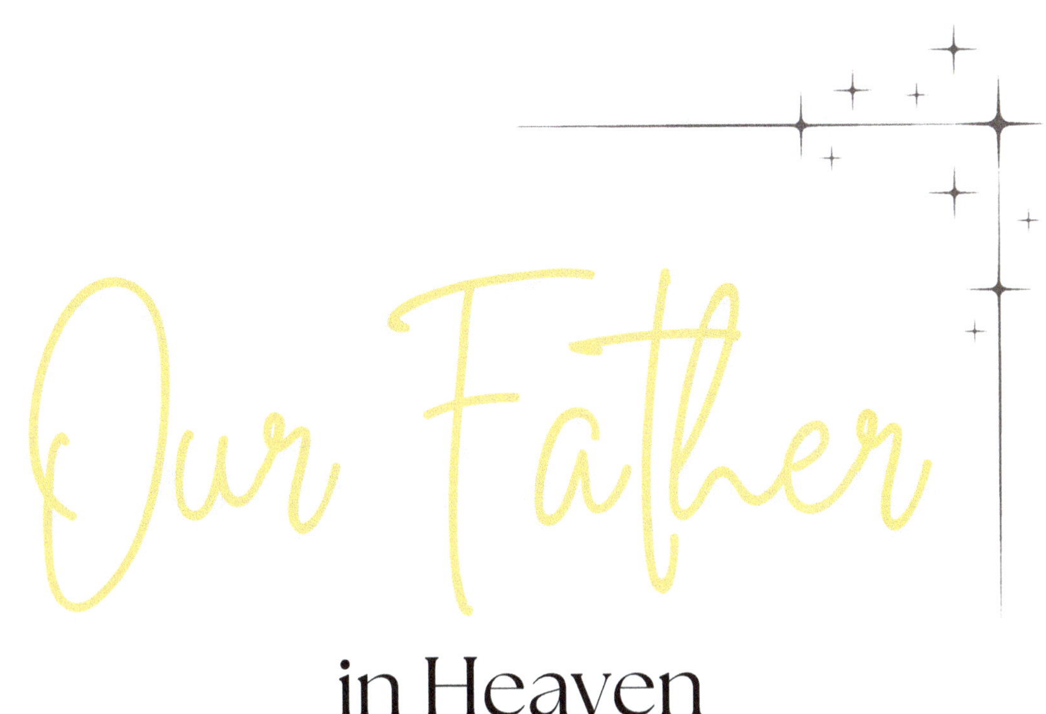

Our Father
in Heaven
Hallowed
be Your
Name

Matthew 6:9

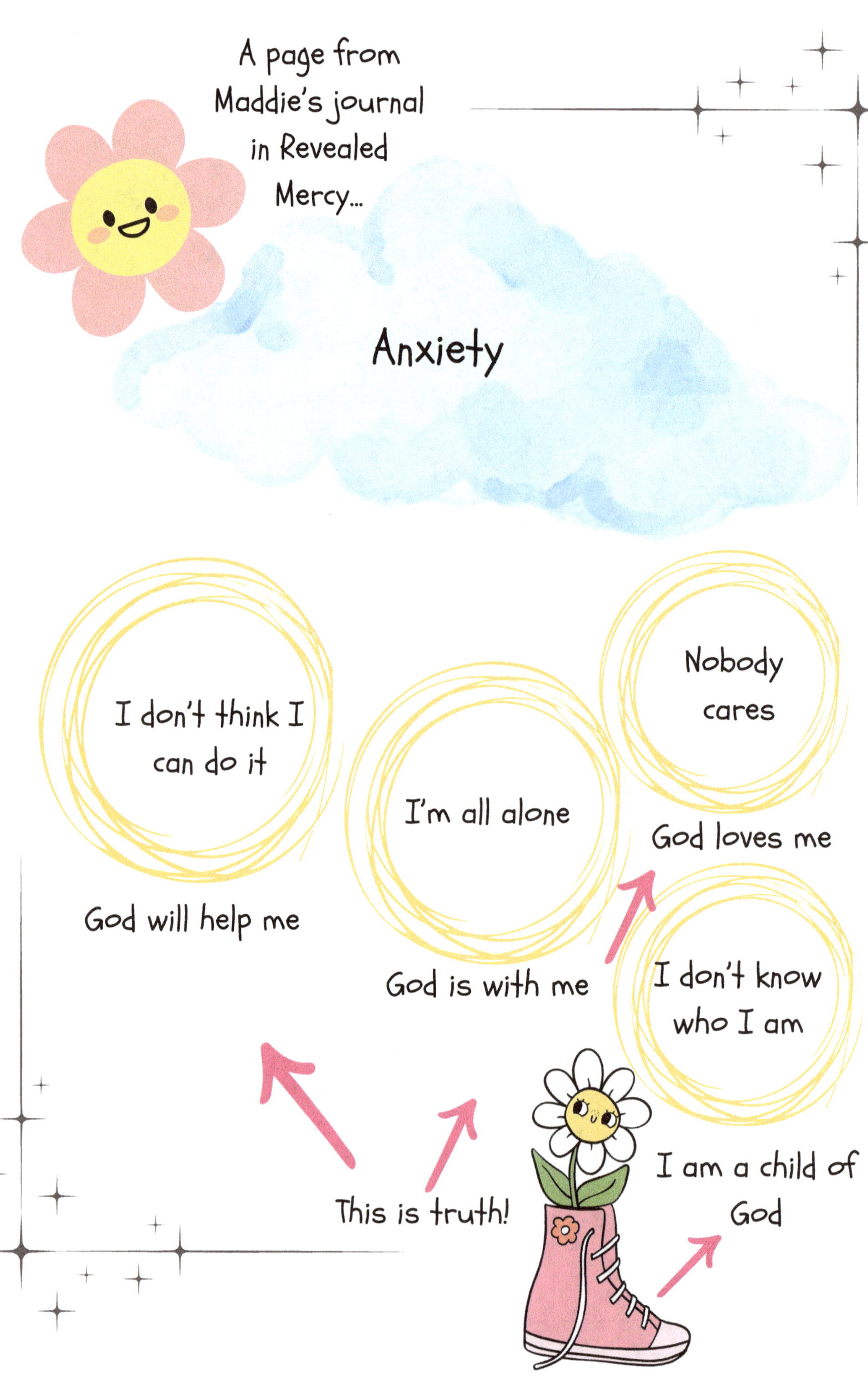

A page from Maddie's journal in Revealed Mercy...
Anxiety
I don't think I can do it
God will help me
I'm all alone
God is with me
Nobody cares
God loves me
I don't know who I am
I am a child of God
This is truth!

Adoration

- Father God I praise You. You have given me life
- and blessed me with friends and family who love me
- You are a good, good Father and you love me, too.
-

Confession

- God, I confess that I've been stuck in my thoughts.
- I haven't been nice to my mom and I've ignored my brother
- Please help me to replace the lies I believe with truth
- and to love others like you love me.

Thanksgiving

- Thank you for my friends and family
- and especially Rachel, Sonya and Grammy
- who taught me how to pray.
-

Supplication

- God, please bless my friends and family and keep us safe
- and help me dad, he's really worried about this hearing..
- Thank you God, I love you.
- Maddie

Today's Scripture

2 Corinthians 10:5
We take captive every thought to make it obedient to Christ

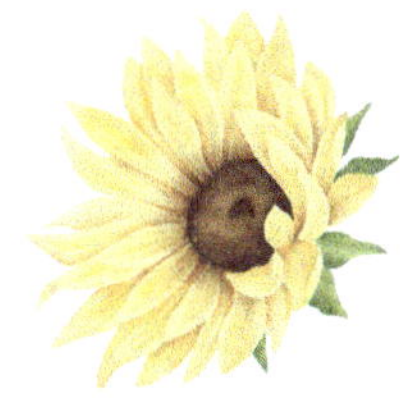

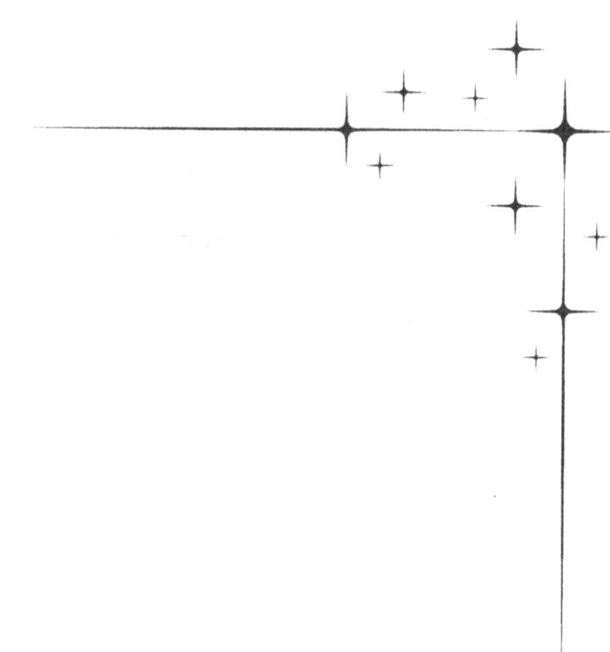
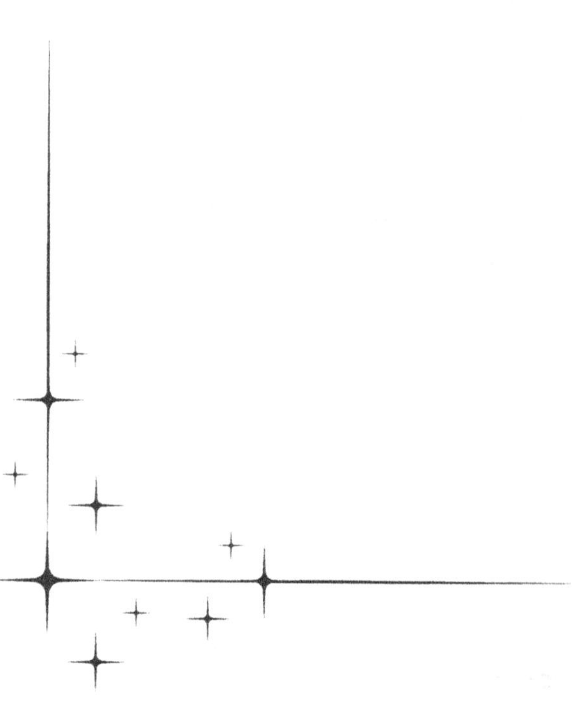

Adoration

- ....
- ....
- ....
- ....

Confession

- ....
- ....
- ....
- ....

Thanksgiving

- ....
- ....
- ....
- ....

Supplication

- ....
- ....
- ....
- ....

Today's Scripture

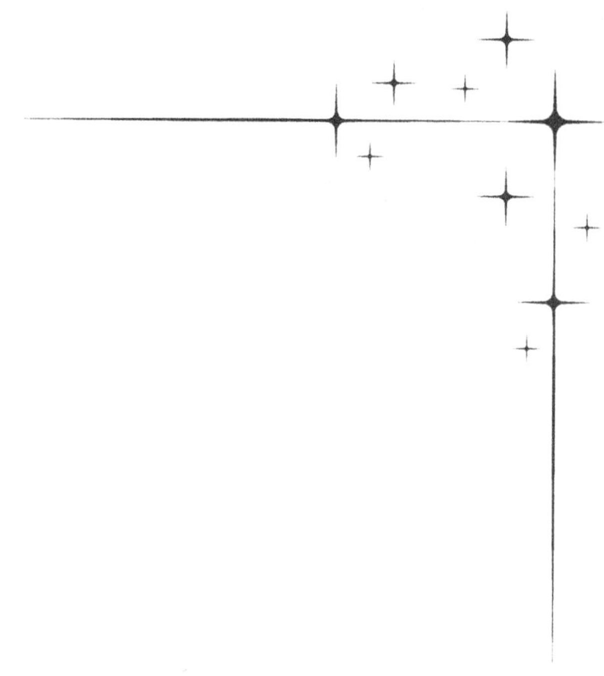
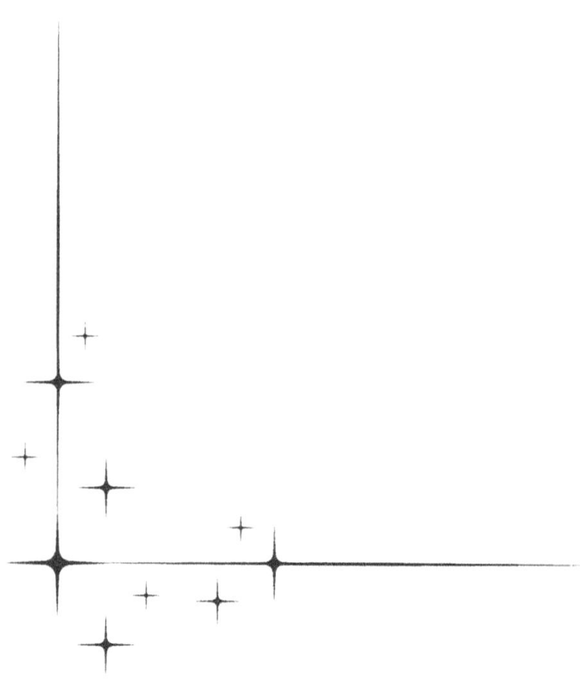

Date: ../../....

Adoration

- ....
- ....
- ....
- ....

Confession

- ....
- ....
- ....
- ....

Thanksgiving

- ....
- ....
- ....
- ....

Supplication

- ....
- ....
- ....
- ....

Today's Scripture

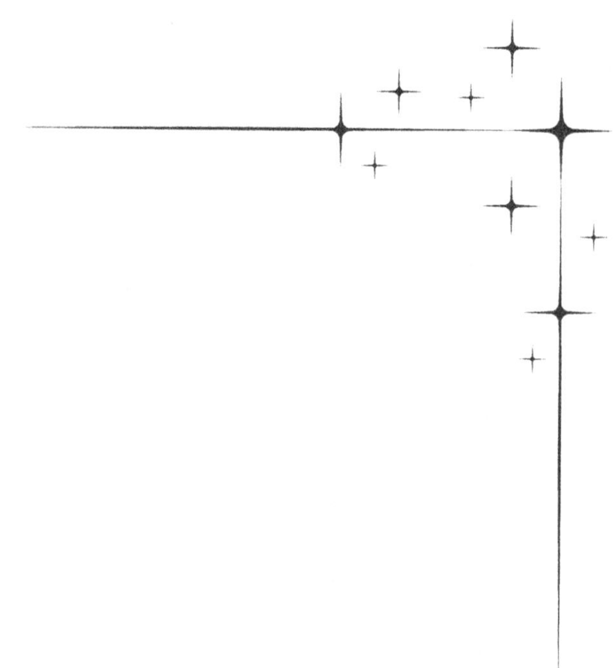
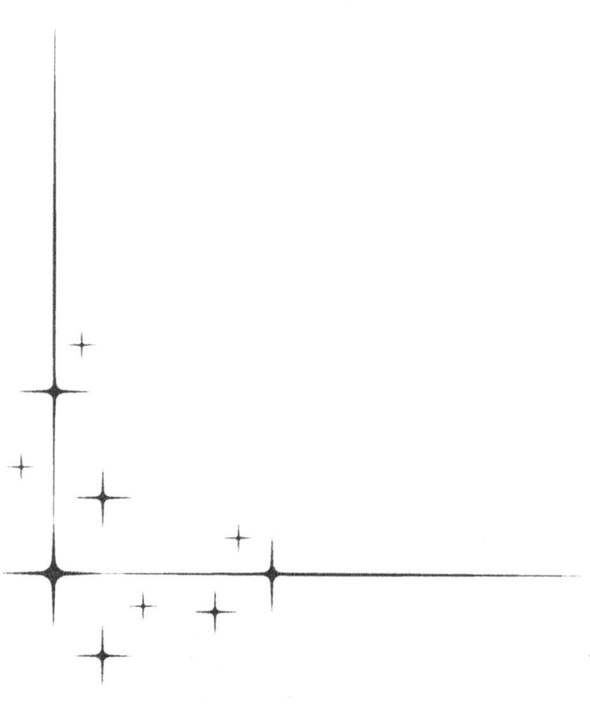

Date: ../../....

Adoration

- ....
- ....
- ....
- ....

Confession

- ....
- ....
- ....
- ....

Thanksgiving

- ....
- ....
- ....
- ....

Supplication

- ....
- ....
- ....
- ....

Today's Scripture

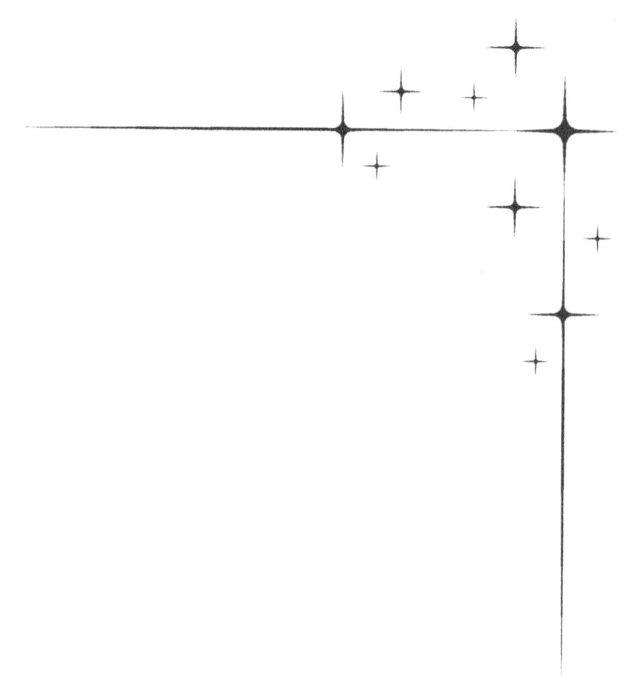
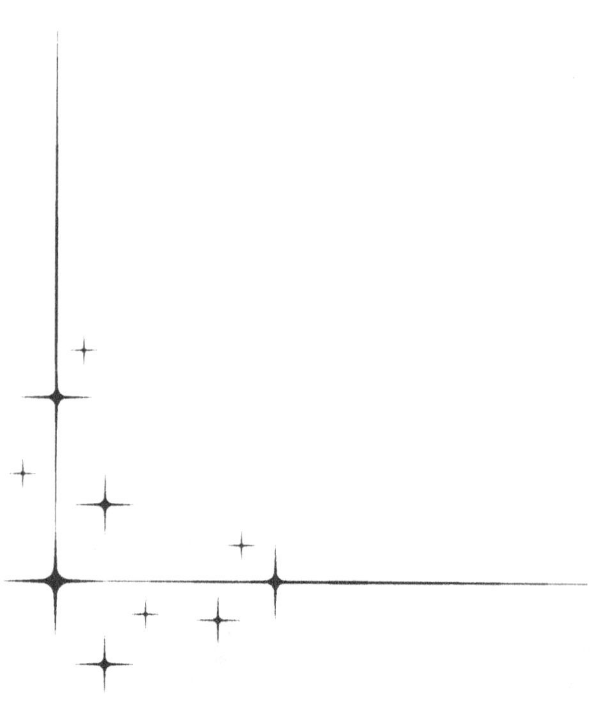

Date: ../../....

Adoration

- ....
- ....
- ....
- ....

Confession

- ....
- ....
- ....
- ....

Thanksgiving

- ....
- ....
- ....
- ....

Supplication

- ....
- ....
- ....
- ....

Today's Scripture

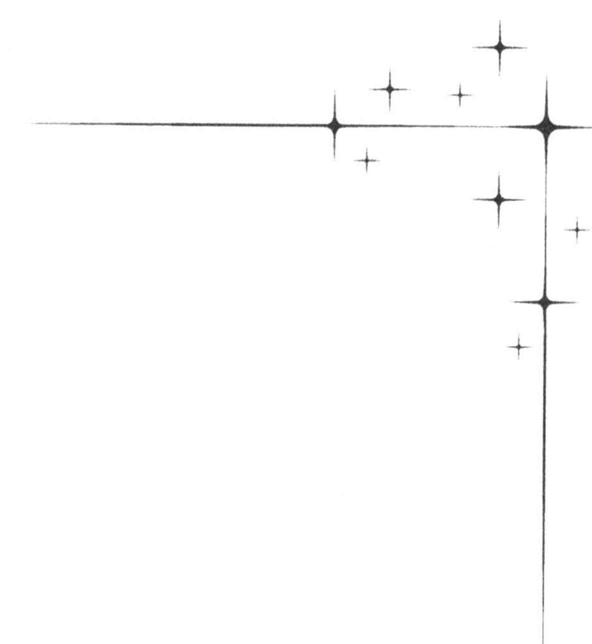
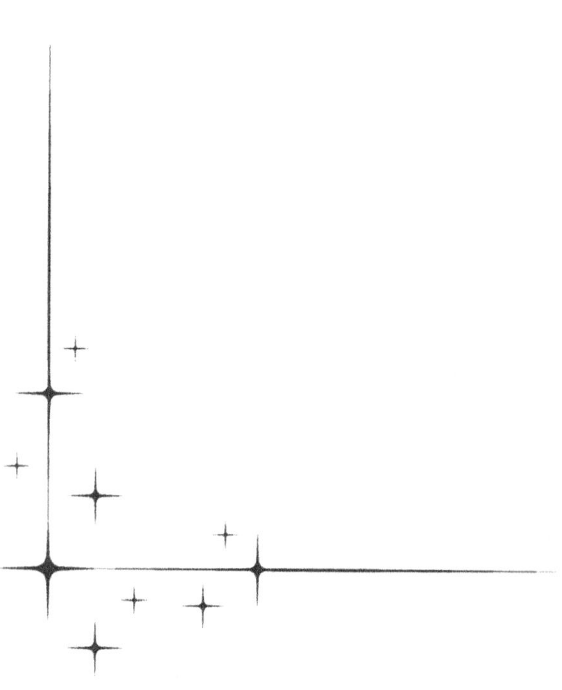

Date: ../../....

Adoration

- ....
- ....
- ....
- ....

Confession

- ....
- ....
- ....
- ....

Thanksgiving

- ....
- ....
- ....
- ....

Supplication

- ....
- ....
- ....
- ....

Today's Scripture

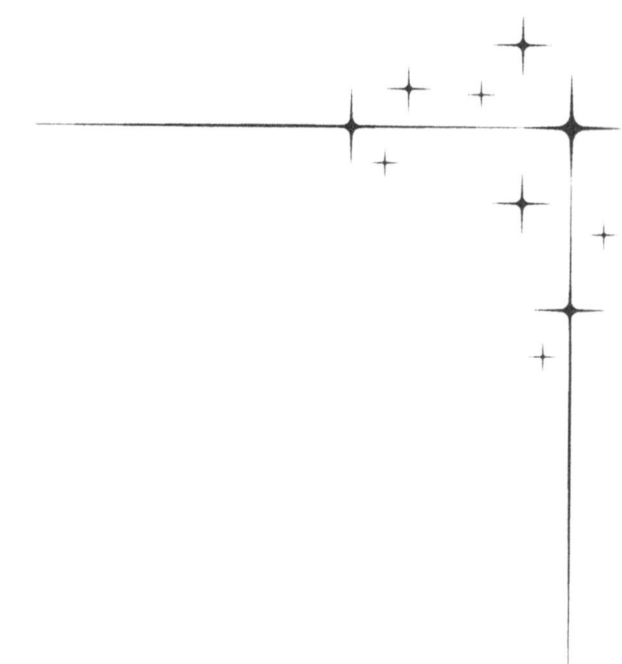

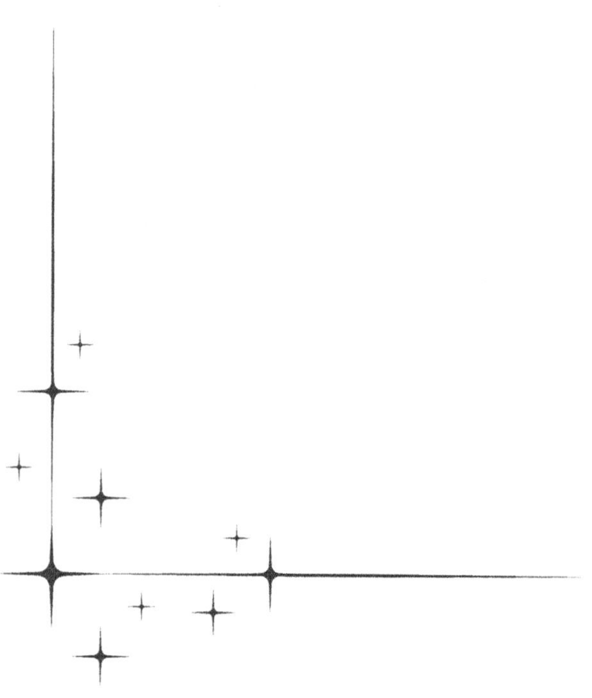

Adoration

- ....

- ....

- ....

- ....

Confession

- ....

- ....

- ....

- ....

Thanksgiving

- ....

- ....

- ....

- ....

Supplication

- ....

- ....

- ....

- ....

Today's Scripture

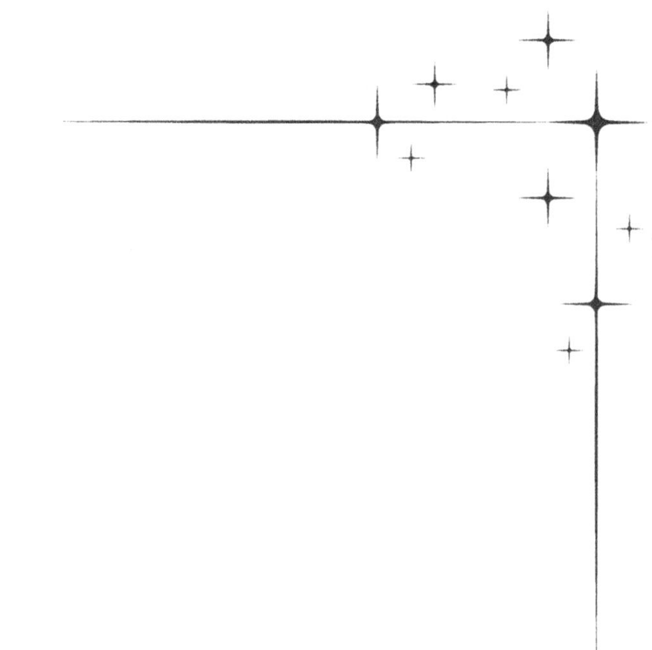
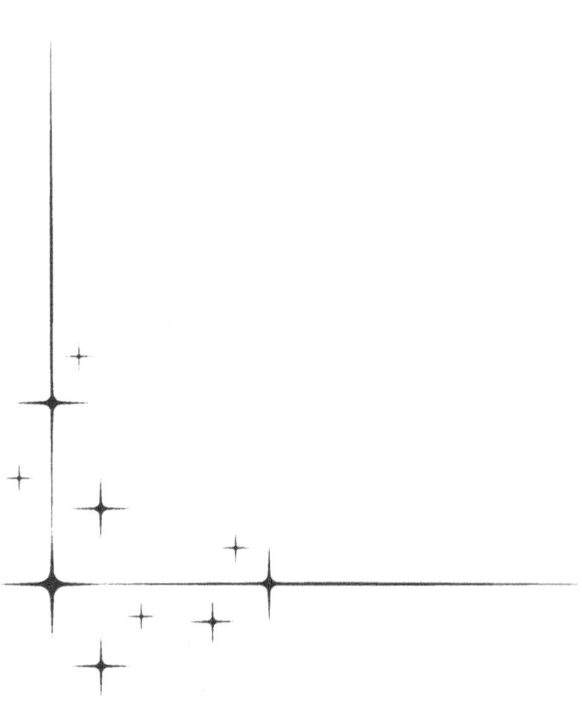

Adoration

- ....
- ....
- ....
- ....

Confession

- ....
- ....
- ....
- ....

Thanksgiving

- ....
- ....
- ....
- ....

Supplication

- ....
- ....
- ....
- ....

Today's Scripture

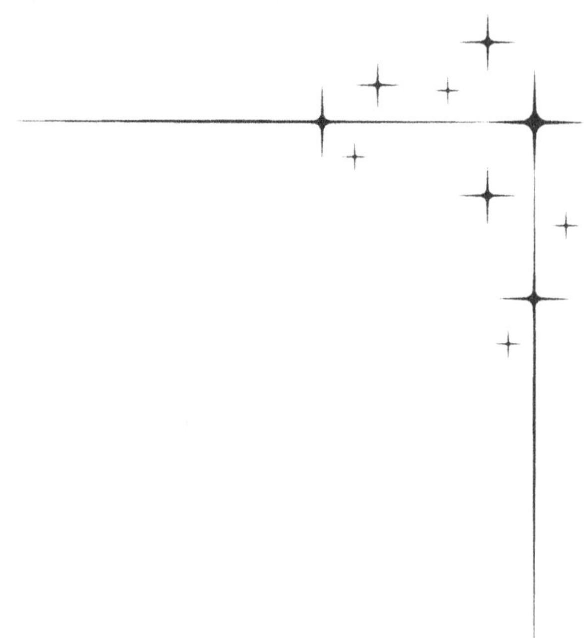

Date: ../../....

Adoration

- ....
- ....
- ....
- ....

Confession

- ....
- ....
- ....
- ....

Thanksgiving

- ....
- ....
- ....
- ....

Supplication

- ....
- ....
- ....
- ....

Today's Scripture

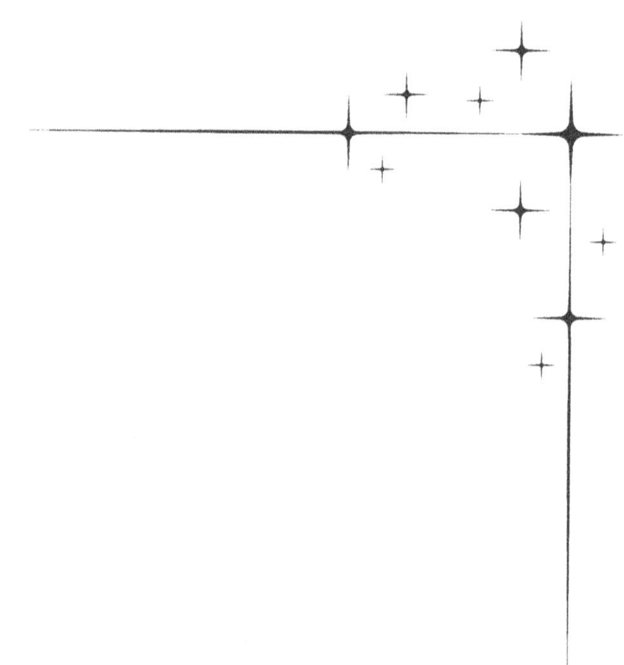
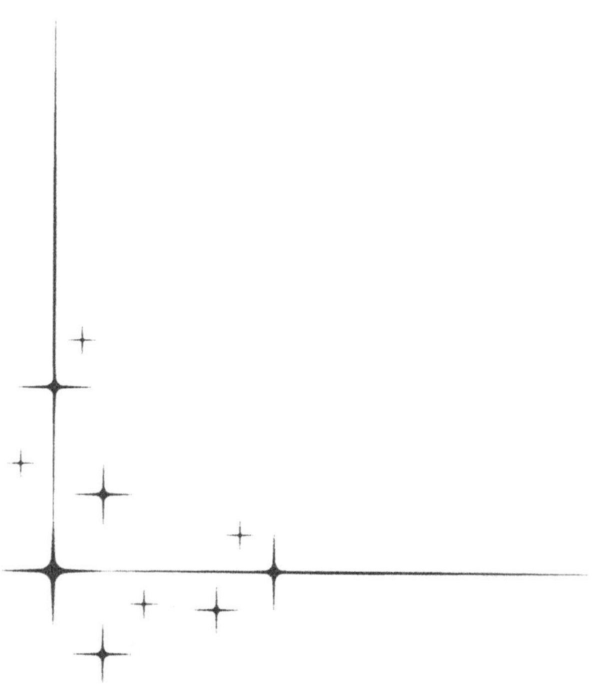

Adoration

- ....
- ....
- ....
- ....

Confession

- ....
- ....
- ....
- ....

Thanksgiving

- ....
- ....
- ....
- ....

Supplication

- ....
- ....
- ....
- ....

Today's Scripture

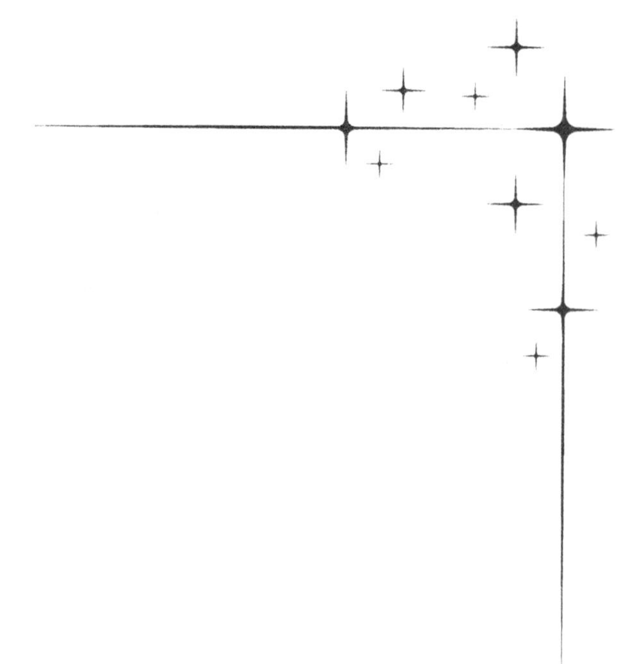
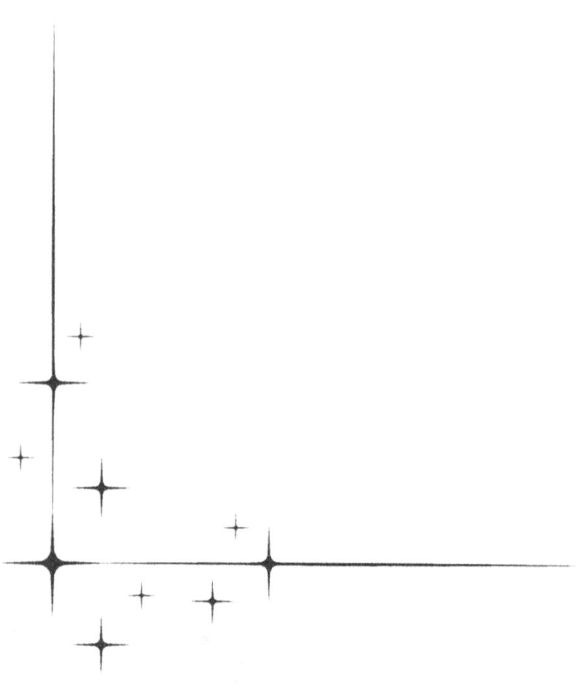

Date: ../../....

Adoration

- ....
- ....
- ....
- ....

Confession

- ....
- ....
- ....
- ....

Thanksgiving

- ....
- ....
- ....
- ....

Supplication

- ....
- ....
- ....
- ....

Today's Scripture

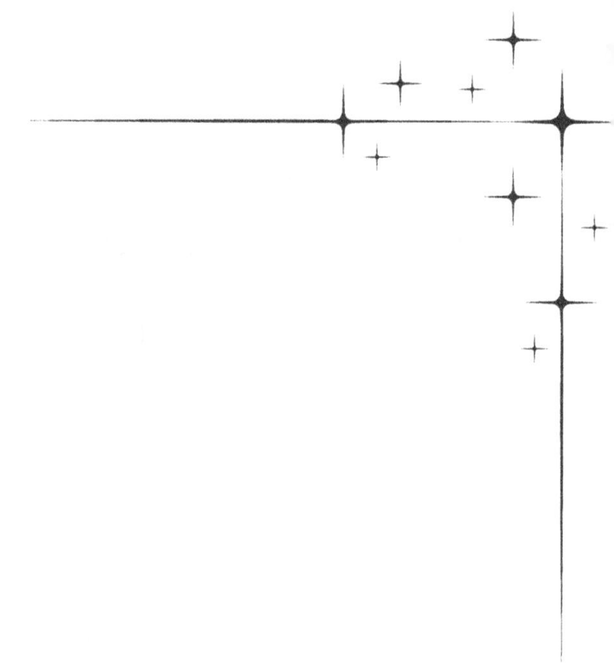
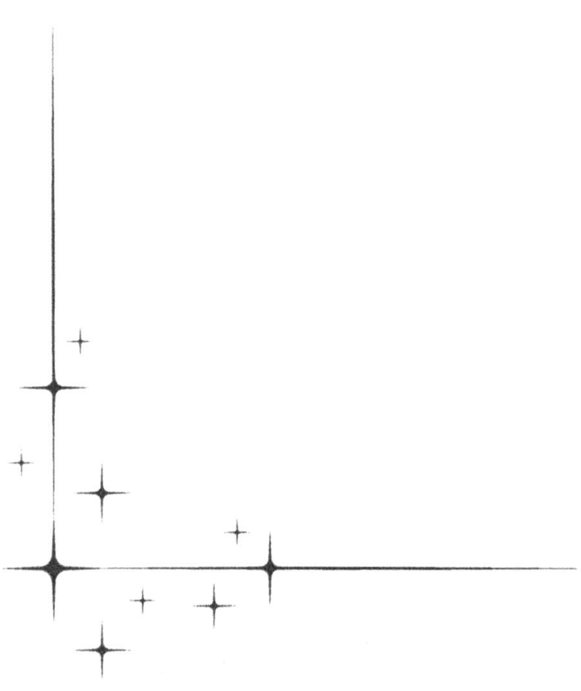

Date: ../../....

Adoration

- ....
- ....
- ....
- ....

Confession

- ....
- ....
- ....
- ....

Thanksgiving

- ....
- ....
- ....
- ....

Supplication

- ....
- ....
- ....
- ....

Today's Scripture

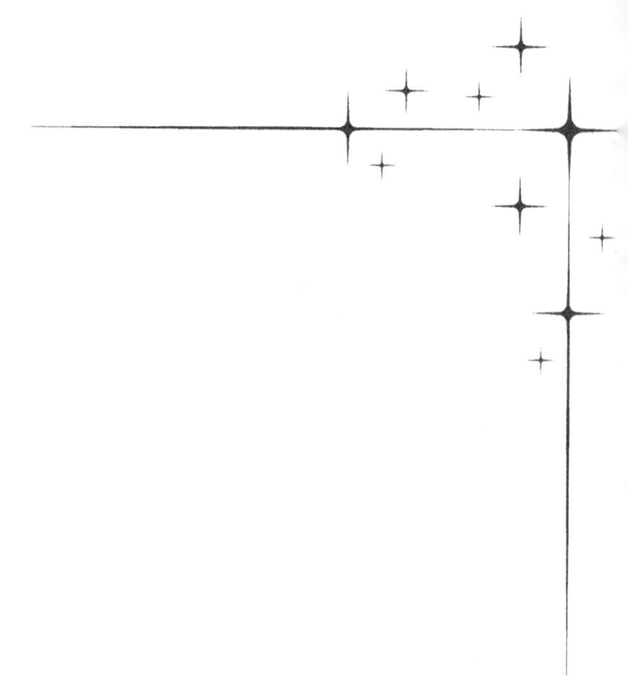
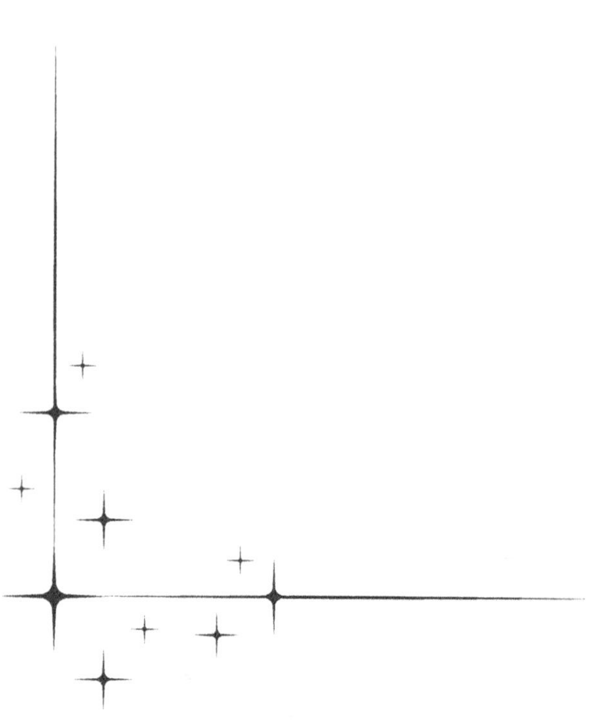

Adoration

- ....
- ....
- ....
- ....

Confession

- ....
- ....
- ....
- ....

Thanksgiving

- ....
- ....
- ....
- ....

Supplication

- ....
- ....
- ....
- ....

Today's Scripture

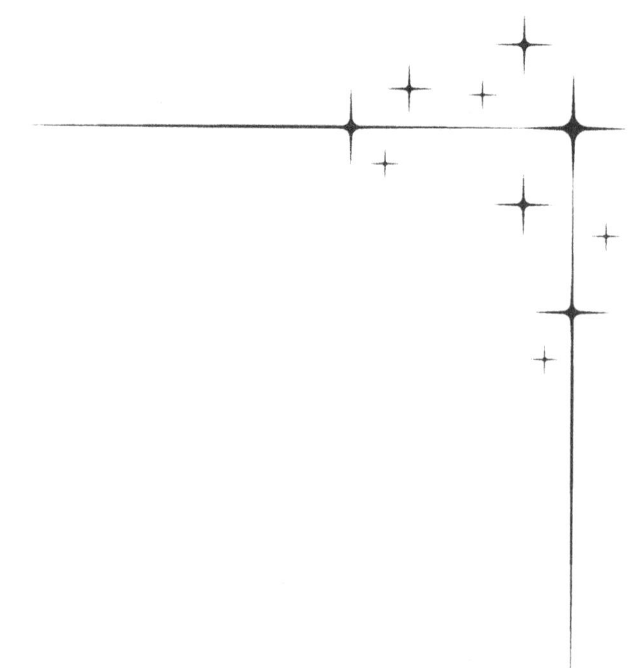

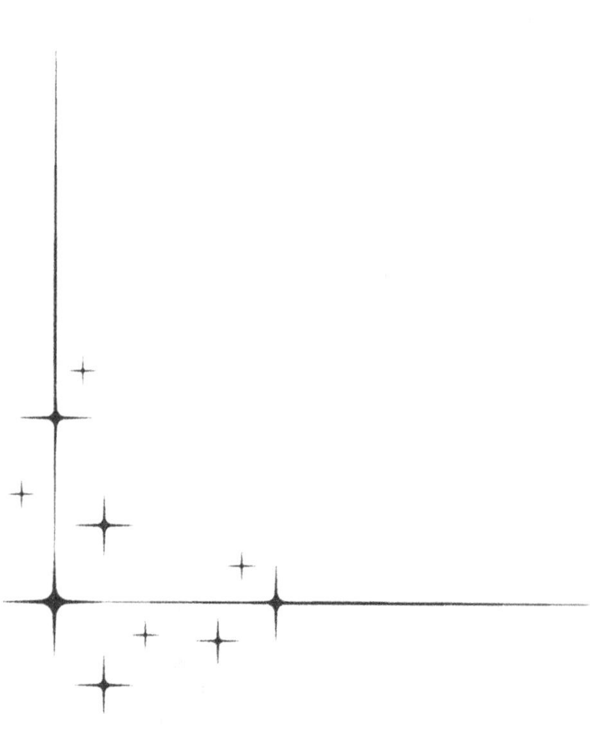

Date: ../../....

Adoration

- ....
- ....
- ....
- ....

Confession

- ....
- ....
- ....
- ....

Thanksgiving

- ....
- ....
- ....
- ....

Supplication

- ....
- ....
- ....
- ....

Today's Scripture

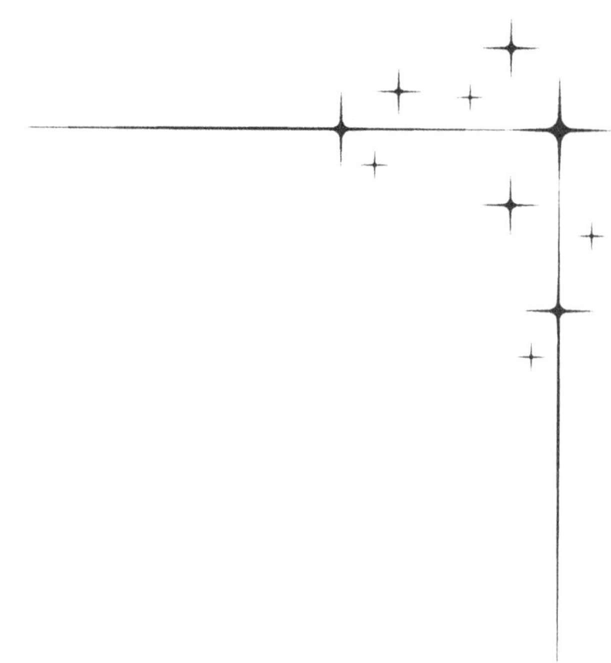
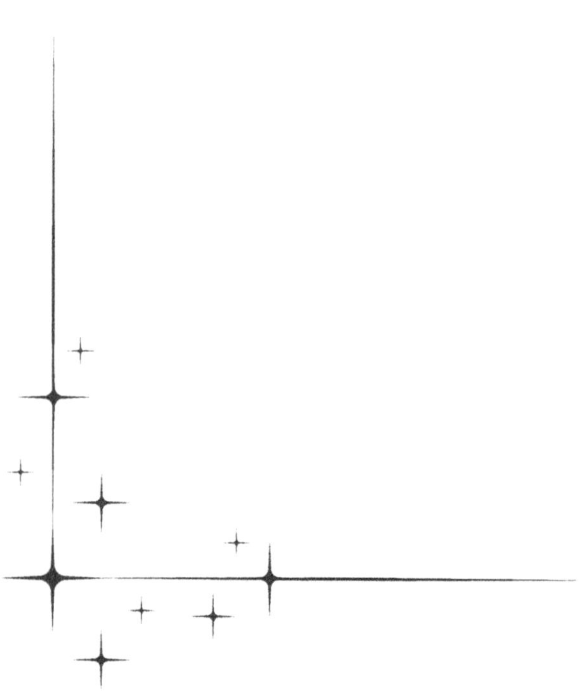

Adoration

- ....
- ....
- ....
- ....

Confession

- ....
- ....
- ....
- ....

Thanksgiving

- ....
- ....
- ....
- ....

Supplication

- ....
- ....
- ....
- ....

Today's Scripture

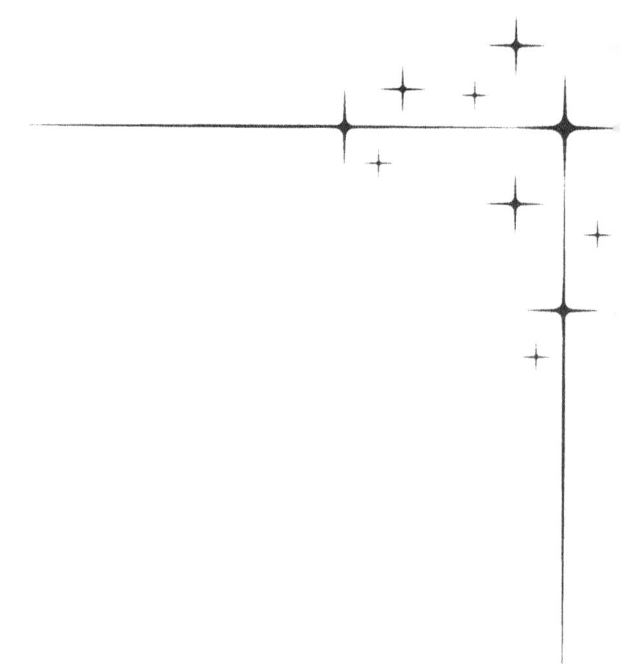
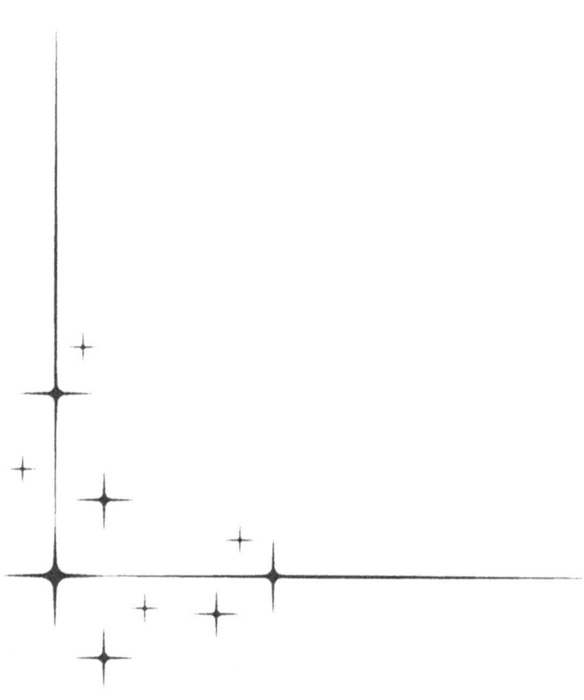

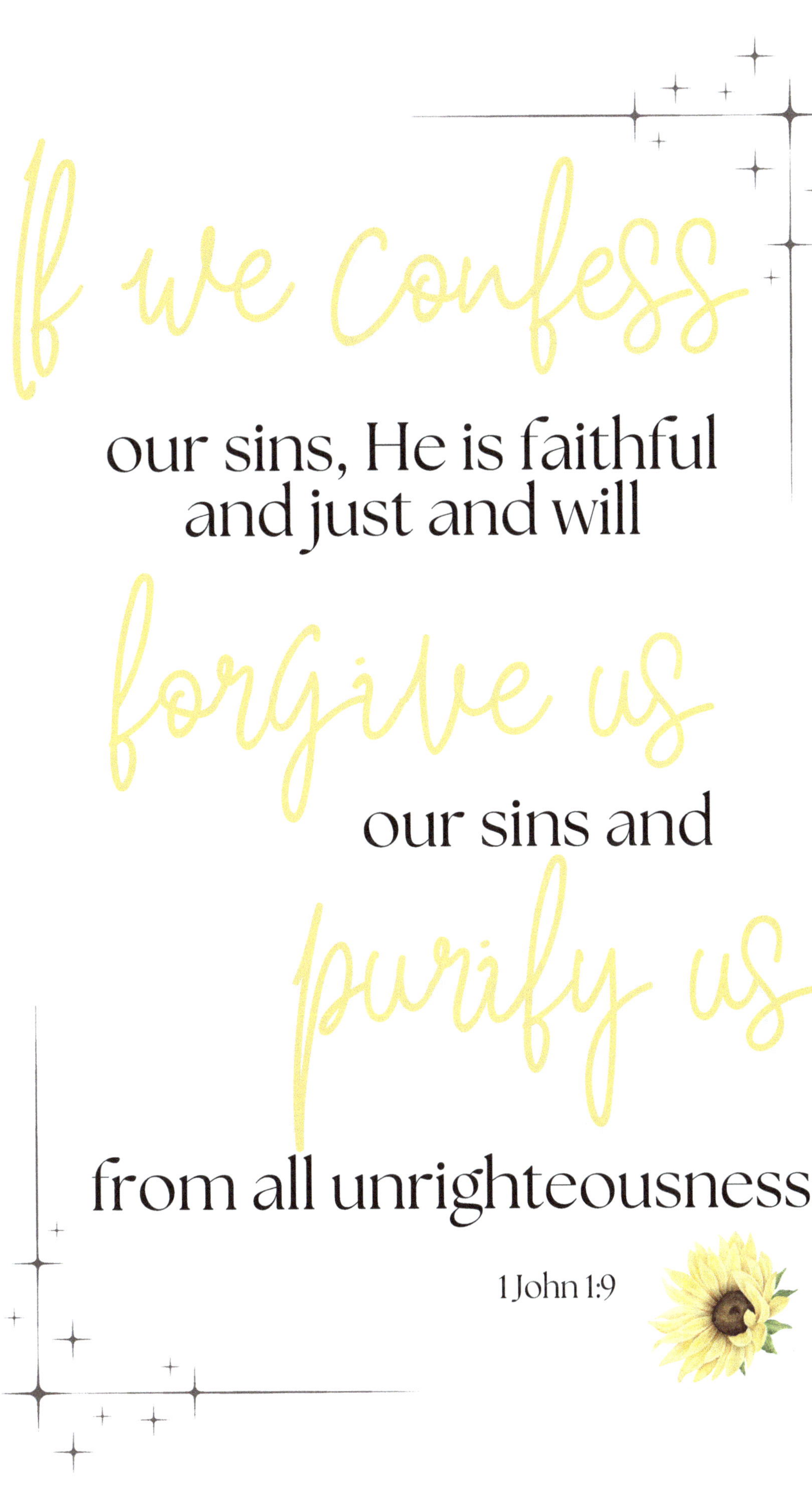

If we confess our sins, He is faithful and just and will forgive us our sins and purify us from all unrighteousness

1 John 1:9

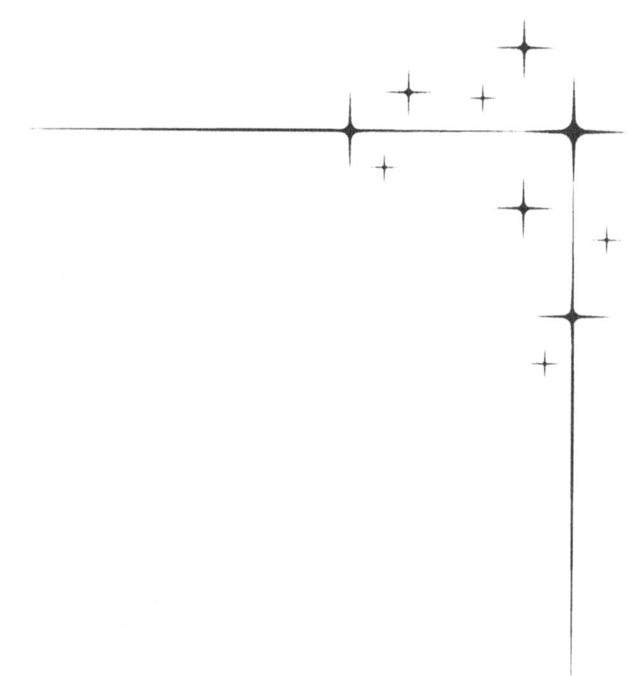

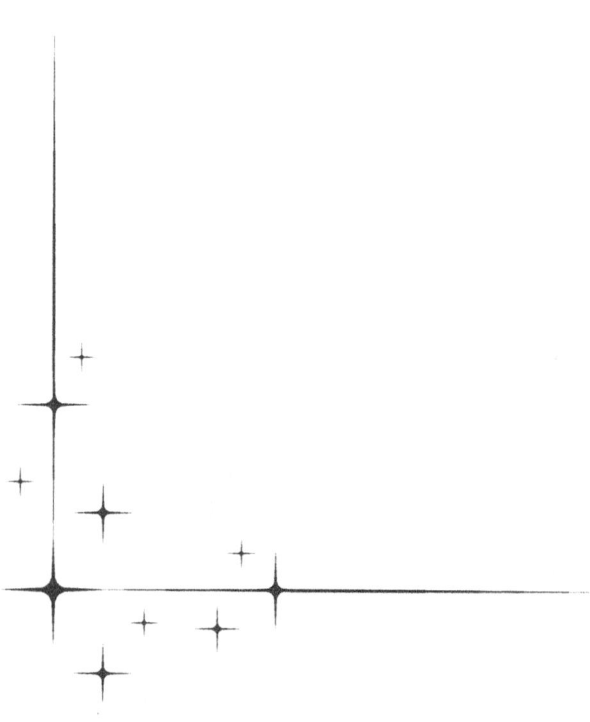

Adoration

- ....
- ....
- ....
- ....

Confession

- ....
- ....
- ....
- ....

Thanksgiving

- ....
- ....
- ....
- ....

Supplication

- ....
- ....
- ....
- ....

Today's Scripture

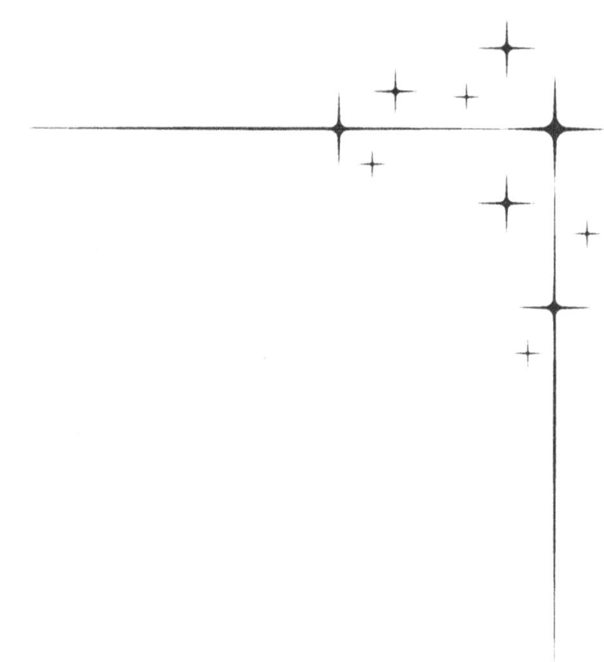
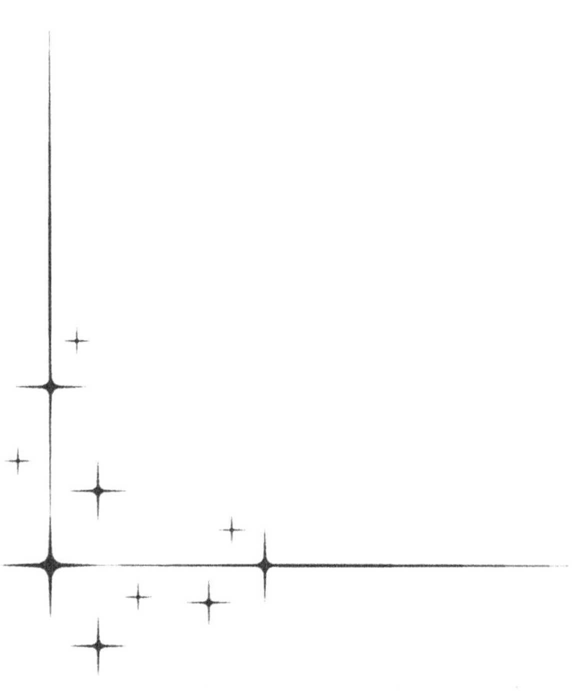

Date: ../../....

Adoration

- ....
- ....
- ....
- ....

Confession

- ....
- ....
- ....
- ....

Thanksgiving

- ....
- ....
- ....
- ....

Supplication

- ....
- ....
- ....
- ....

Today's Scripture

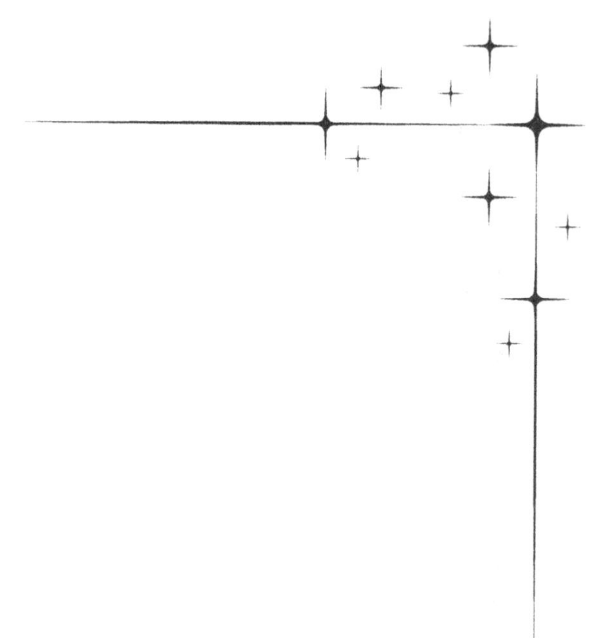
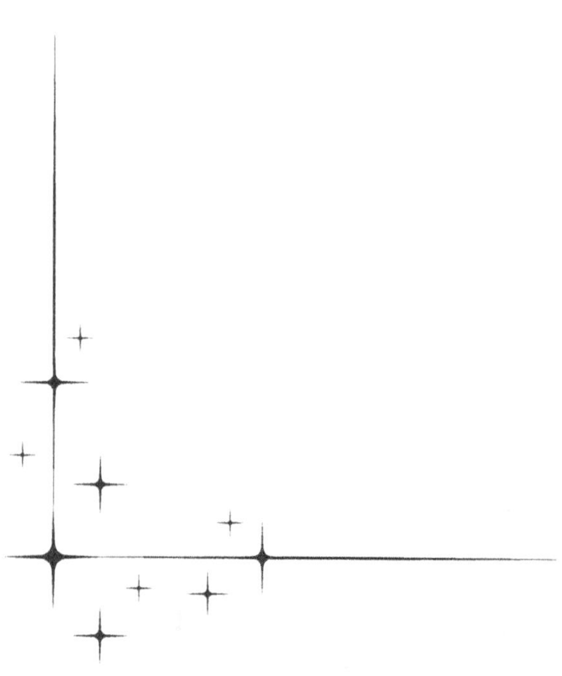

Date: ../../....

Adoration

- ....
- ....
- ....
- ....

Confession

- ....
- ....
- ....
- ....

Thanksgiving

- ....
- ....
- ....
- ....

Supplication

- ....
- ....
- ....
- ....

Today's Scripture

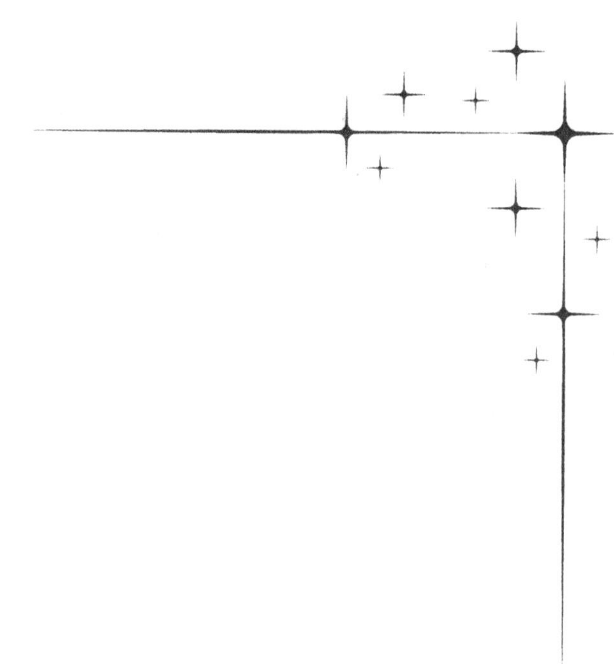
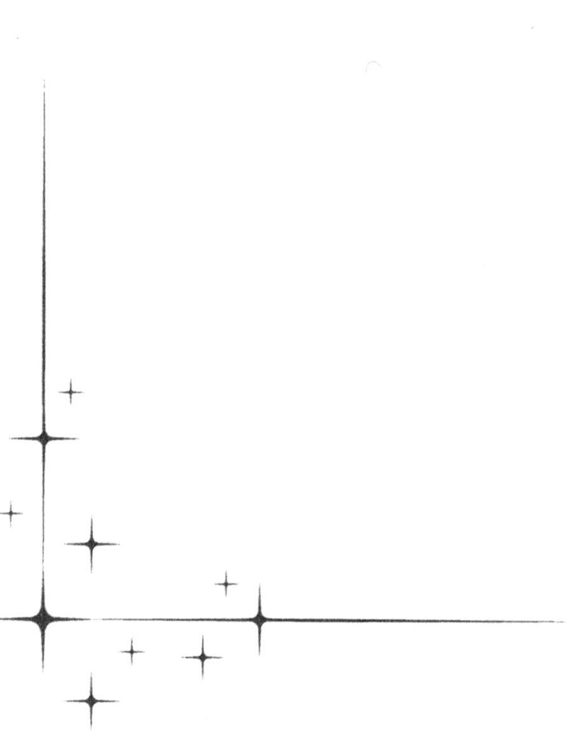

Adoration

- ....
- ....
- ....
- ....

Confession

- ....
- ....
- ....
- ....

Thanksgiving

- ....
- ....
- ....
- ....

Supplication

- ....
- ....
- ....
- ....

Today's Scripture

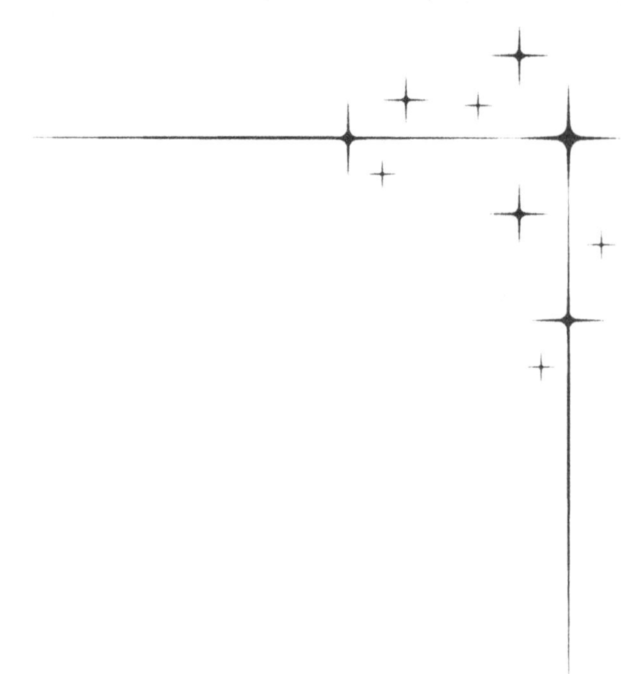
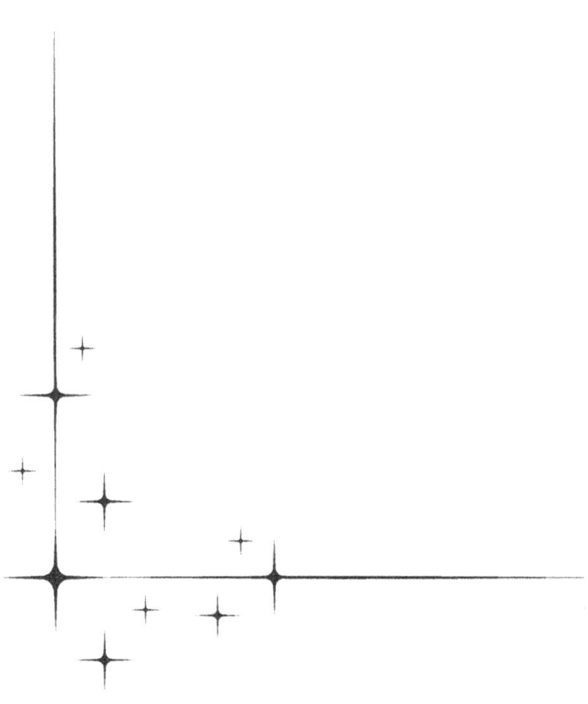

Adoration

- ....
- ....
- ....
- ....

Confession

- ....
- ....
- ....
- ....

Thanksgiving

- ....
- ....
- ....
- ....

Supplication

- ....
- ....
- ....
- ....

Today's Scripture

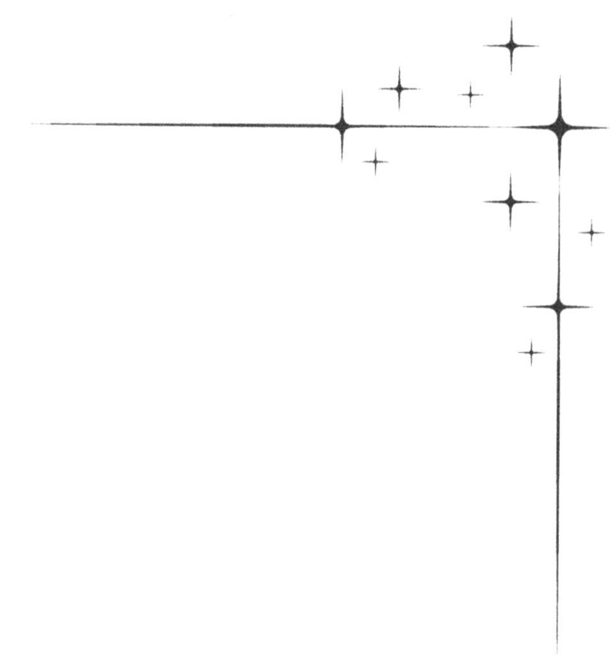
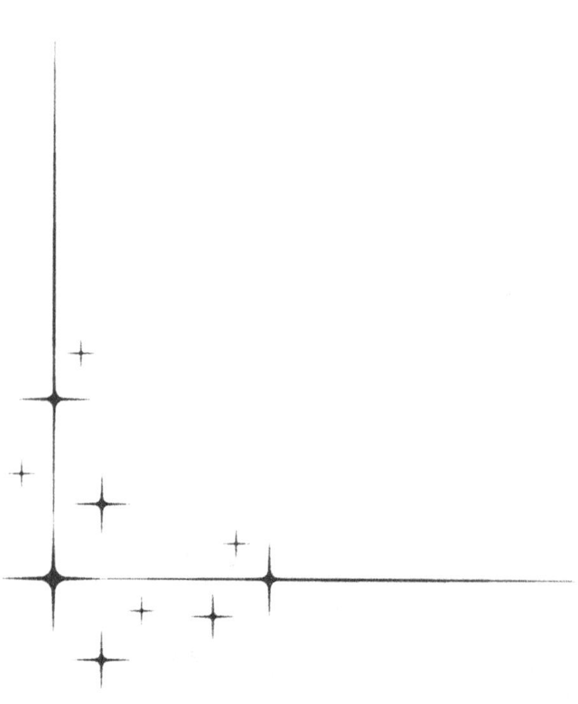

Date: ../../....

Adoration

- ....
- ....
- ....
- ....

Confession

- ....
- ....
- ....
- ....

Thanksgiving

- ....
- ....
- ....
- ....

Supplication

- ....
- ....
- ....
- ....

Today's Scripture

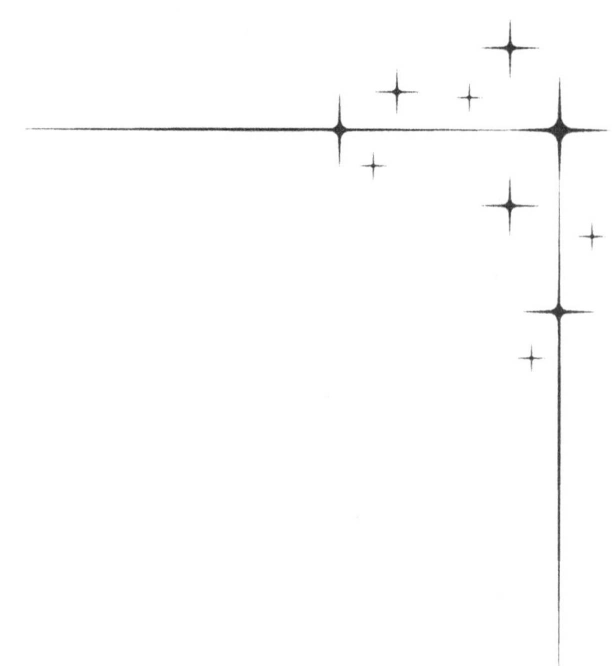
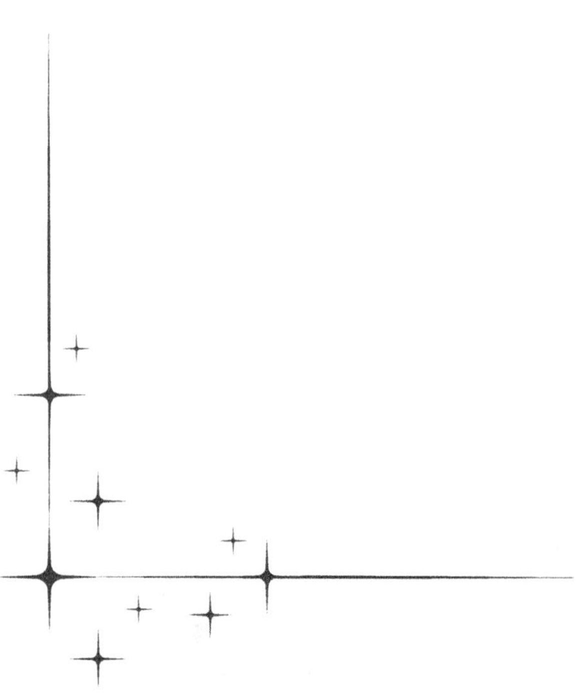

Adoration

- ....
- ....
- ....
- ....

Confession

- ....
- ....
- ....
- ....

Thanksgiving

- ....
- ....
- ....
- ....

Supplication

- ....
- ....
- ....
- ....

Today's Scripture

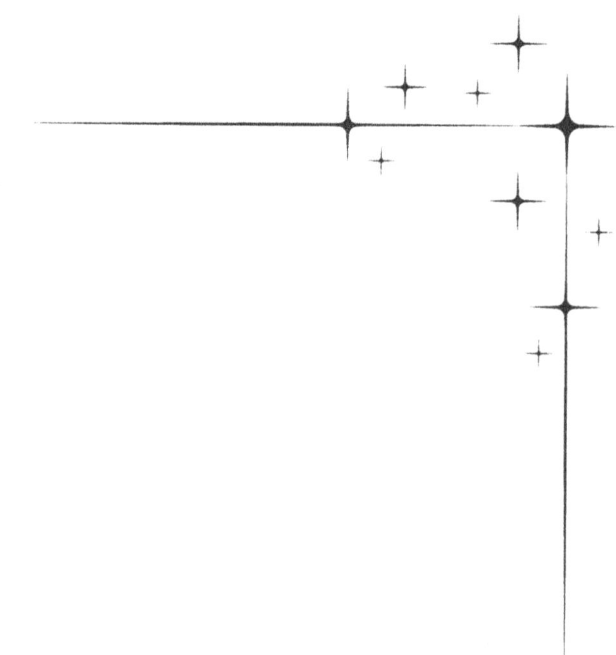
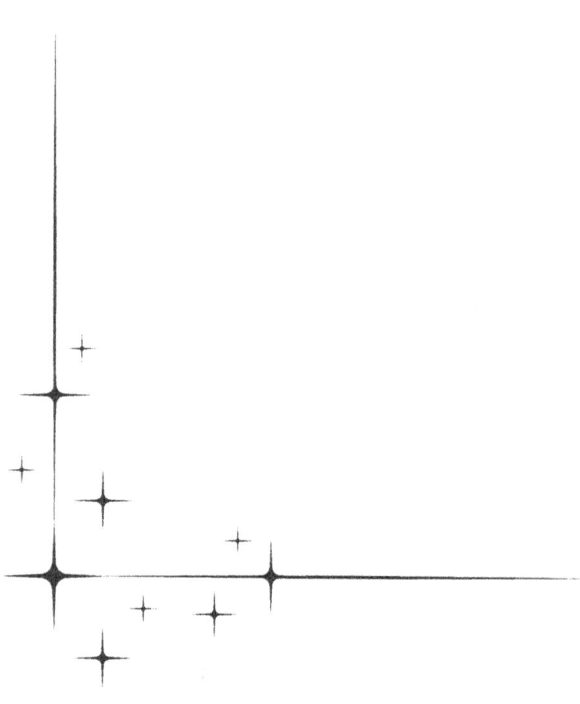

Adoration

- ....
- ....
- ....
- ....

Confession

- ....
- ....
- ....
- ....

Thanksgiving

- ....
- ....
- ....
- ....

Supplication

- ....
- ....
- ....
- ....

Today's Scripture

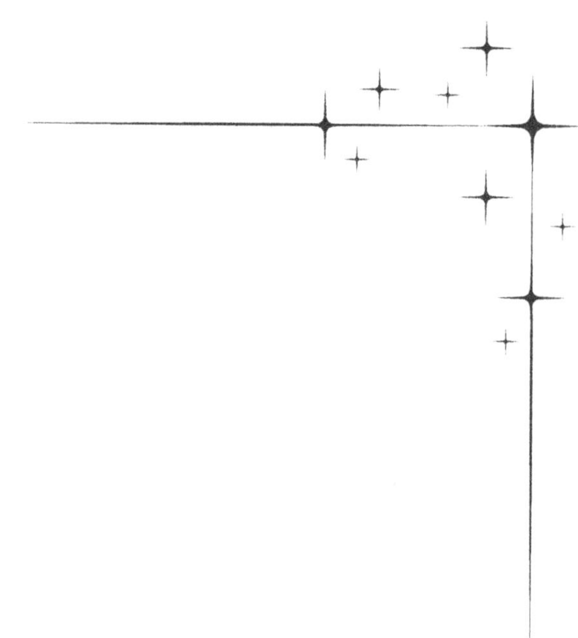
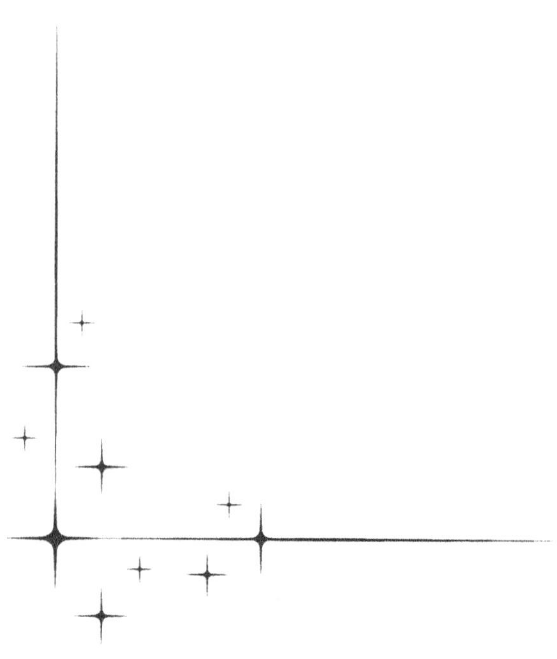

Date: ../../....

Adoration

- ....
- ....
- ....
- ....

Confession

- ....
- ....
- ....
- ....

Thanksgiving

- ....
- ....
- ....
- ....

Supplication

- ....
- ....
- ....
- ....

Today's Scripture

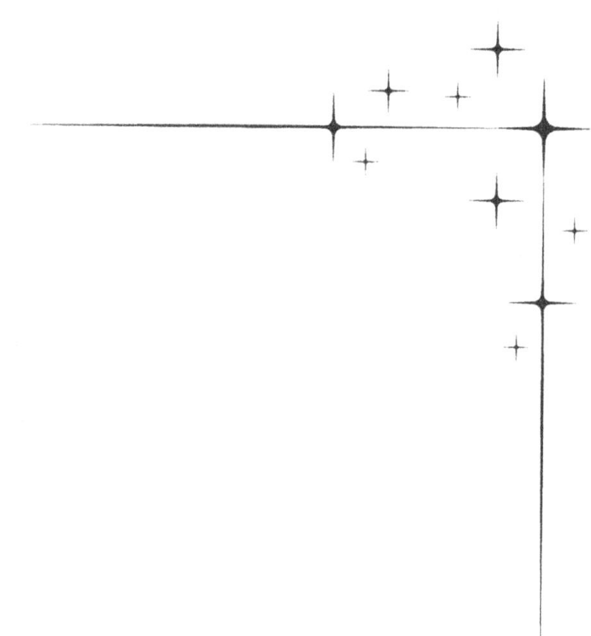

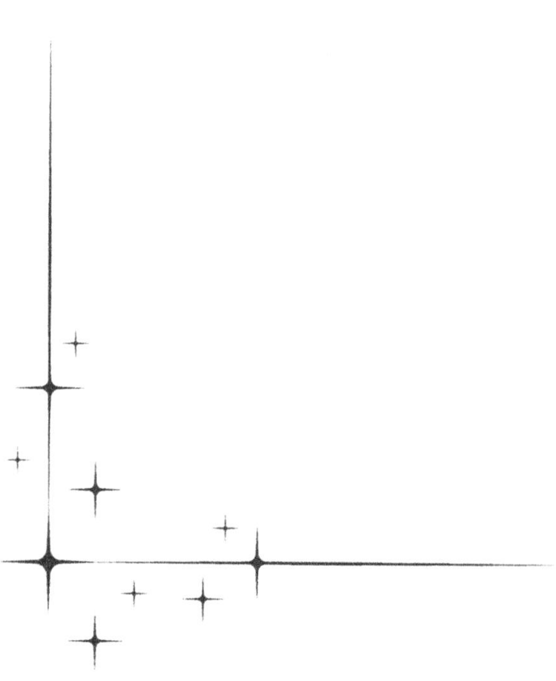

Date: ../../....

Adoration

- ....
- ....
- ....
- ....

Confession

- ....
- ....
- ....
- ....

Thanksgiving

- ....
- ....
- ....
- ....

Supplication

- ....
- ....
- ....
- ....

Today's Scripture

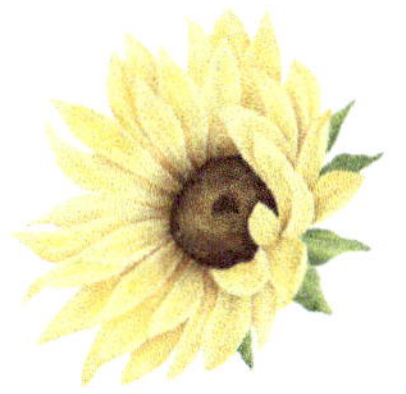

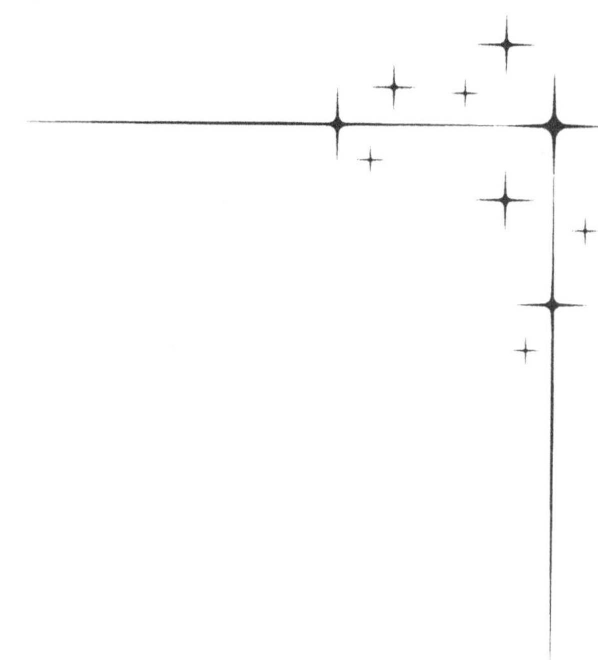

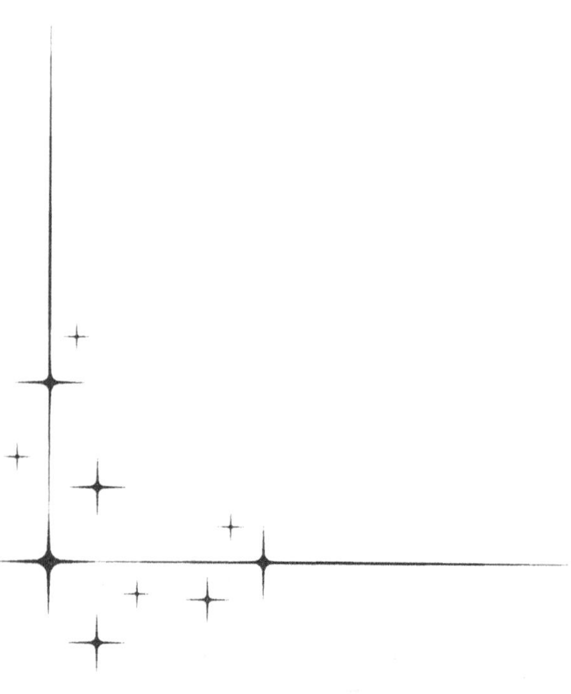

Date: ../../....

Adoration

- ....
- ....
- ....
- ....

Confession

- ....
- ....
- ....
- ....

Thanksgiving

- ....
- ....
- ....
- ....

Supplication

- ....
- ....
- ....
- ....

Today's Scripture

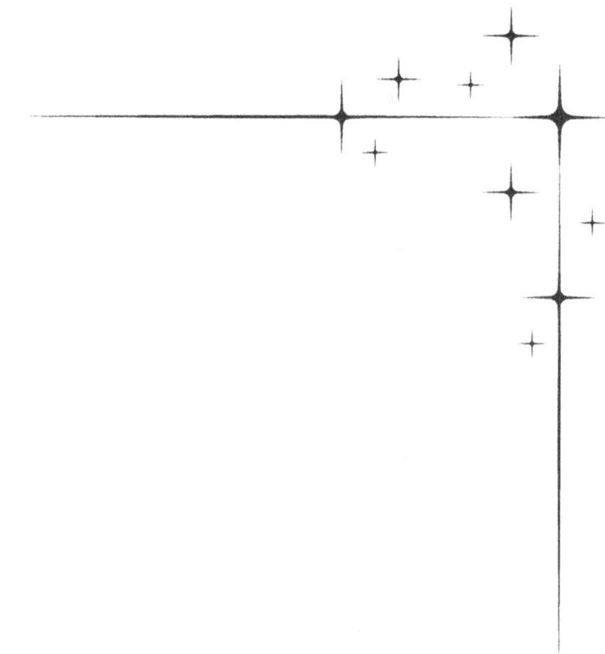
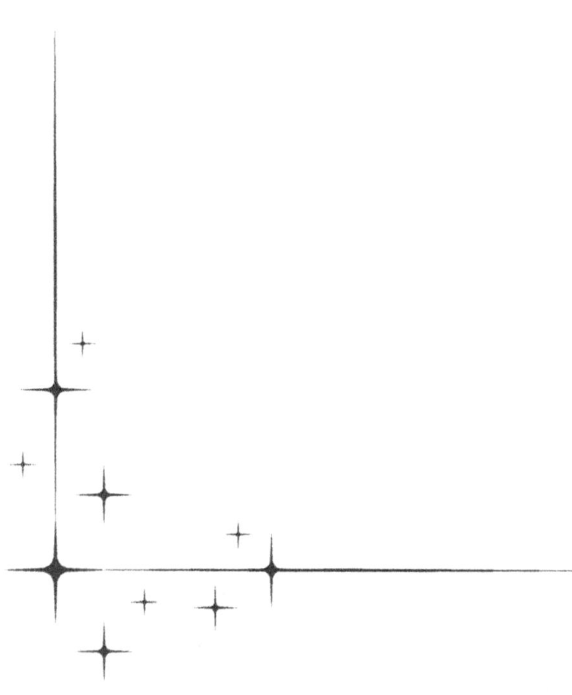

Adoration

- ....
- ....
- ....
- ....

Confession

- ....
- ....
- ....
- ....

Thanksgiving

- ....
- ....
- ....
- ....

Supplication

- ....
- ....
- ....
- ....

Today's Scripture

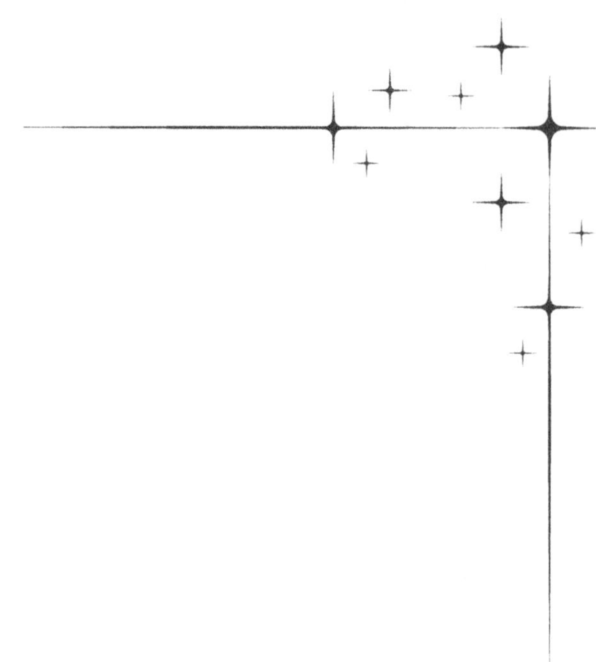

Date: ../../....

Adoration

- ....
- ....
- ....
- ....

Confession

- ....
- ....
- ....
- ....

Thanksgiving

- ....
- ....
- ....
- ....

Supplication

- ....
- ....
- ....
- ....

Today's Scripture

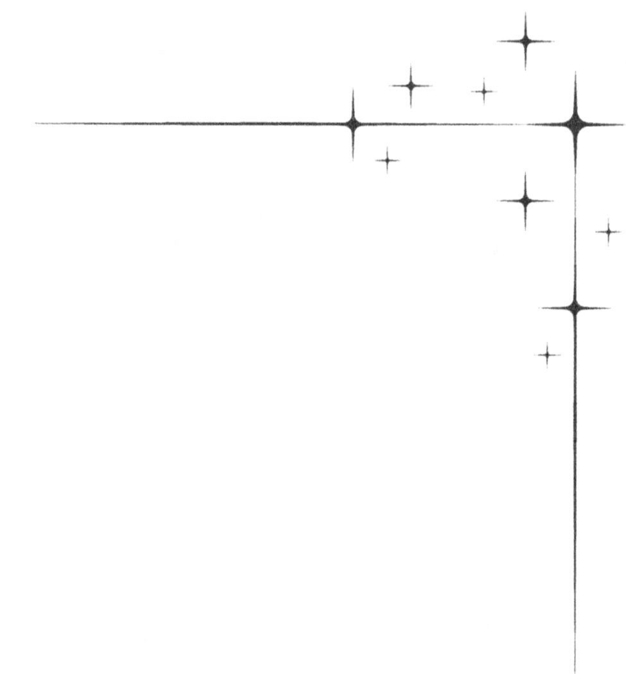
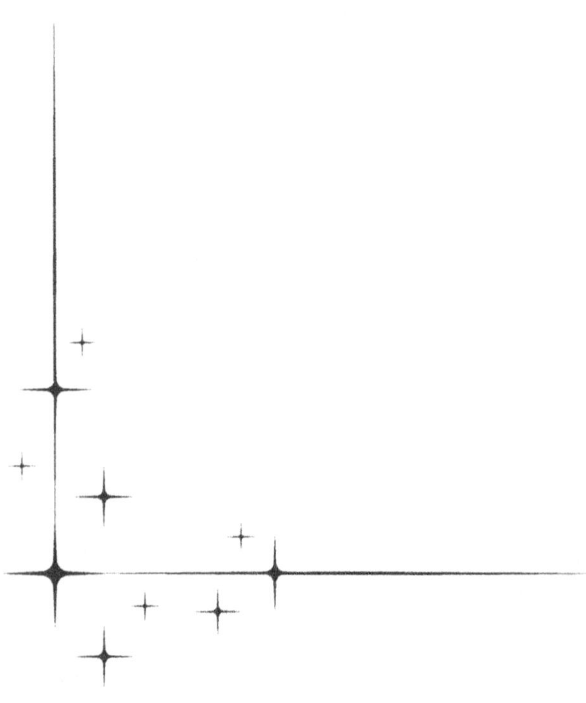

Date: ../../....

Adoration

- ....
- ....
- ....
- ....

Confession

- ....
- ....
- ....
- ....

Thanksgiving

- ....
- ....
- ....
- ....

Supplication

- ....
- ....
- ....
- ....

Today's Scripture

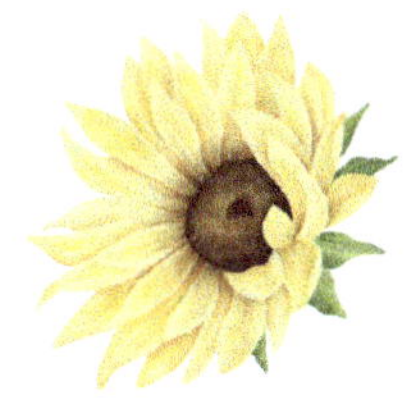

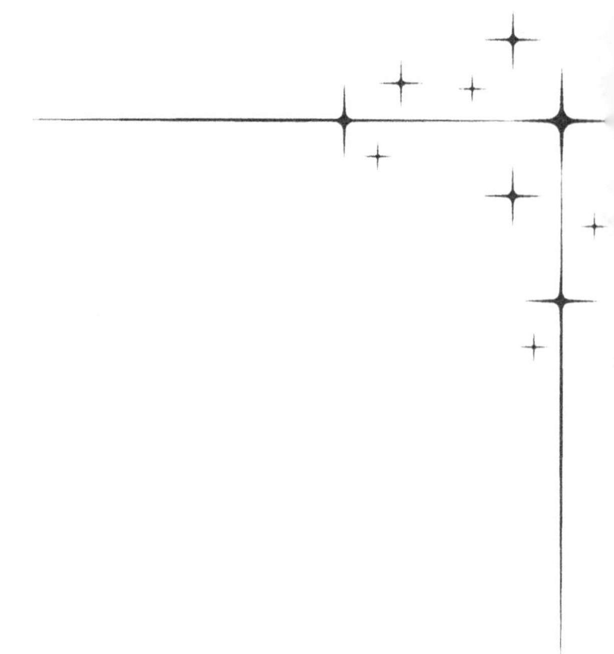
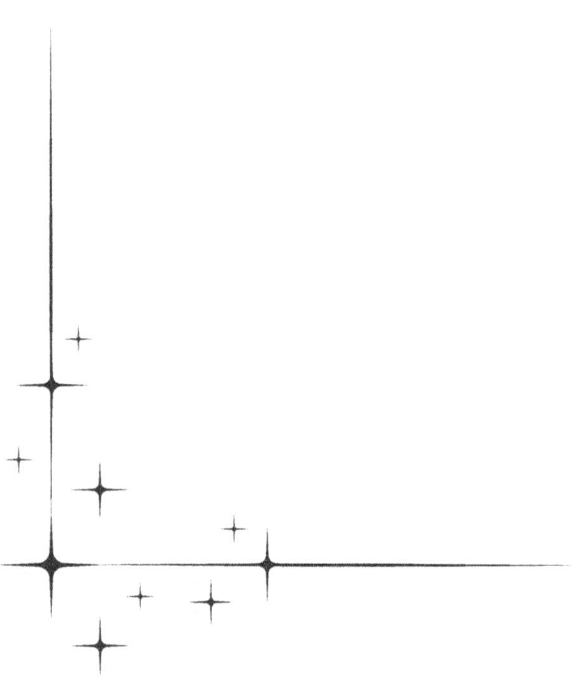

Adoration

- ....
- ....
- ....
- ....

Confession

- ....
- ....
- ....
- ....

Thanksgiving

- ....
- ....
- ....
- ....

Supplication

- ....
- ....
- ....
- ....

Today's Scripture

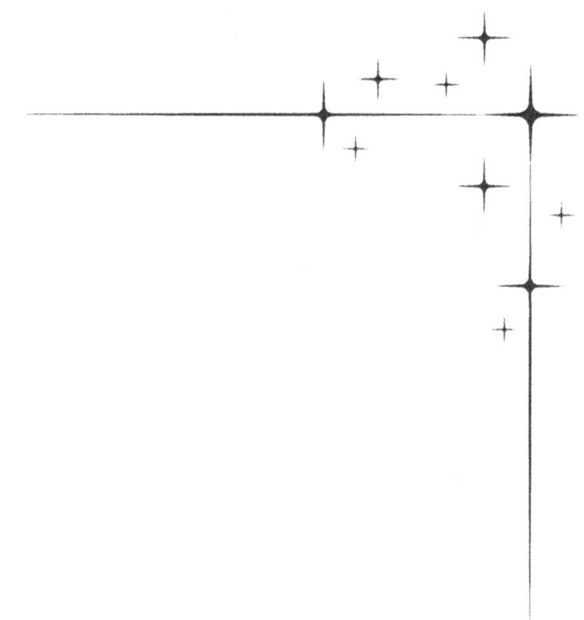

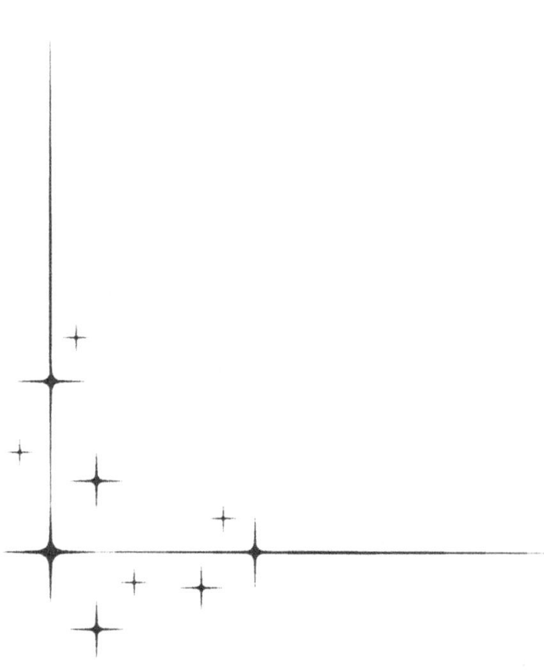

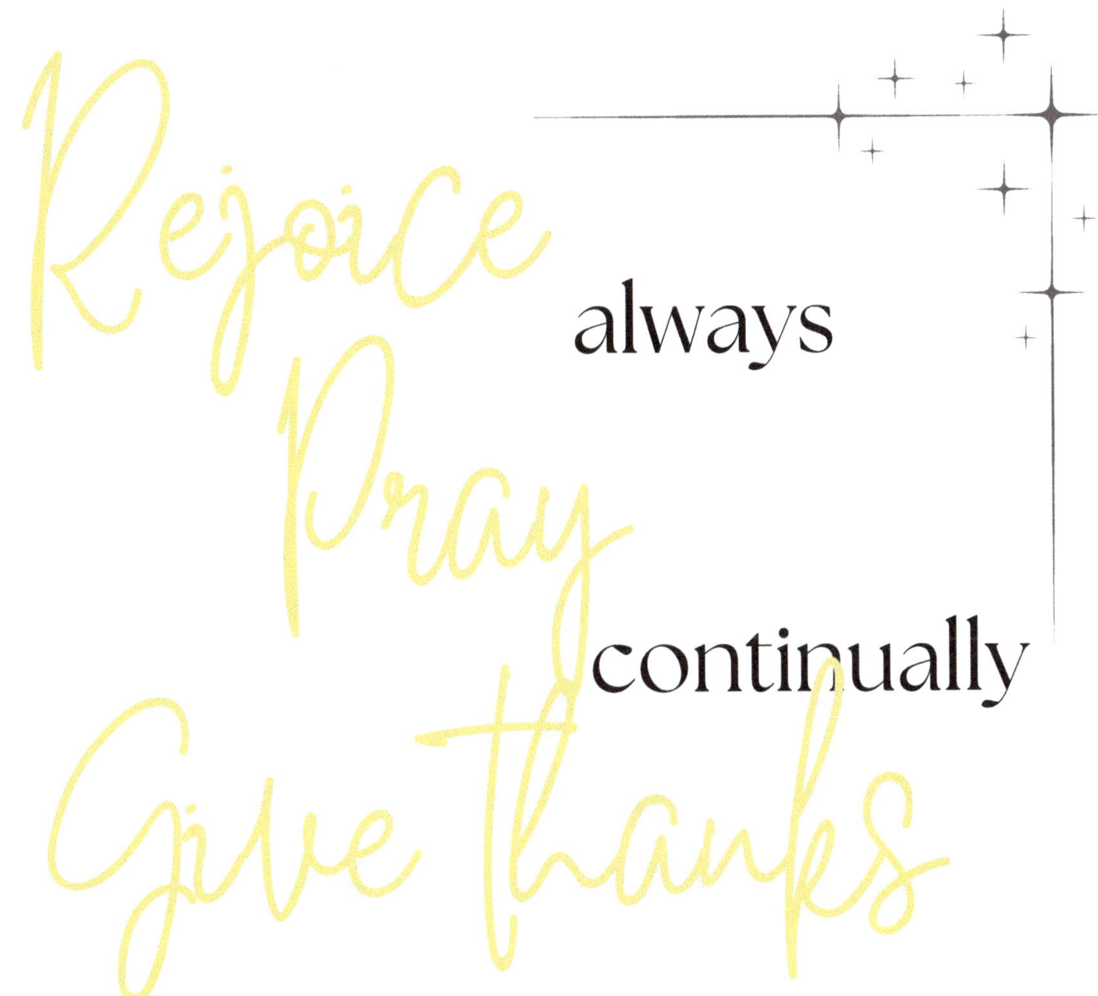

Rejoice always
Pray continually
Give thanks
in all circumstances for this is

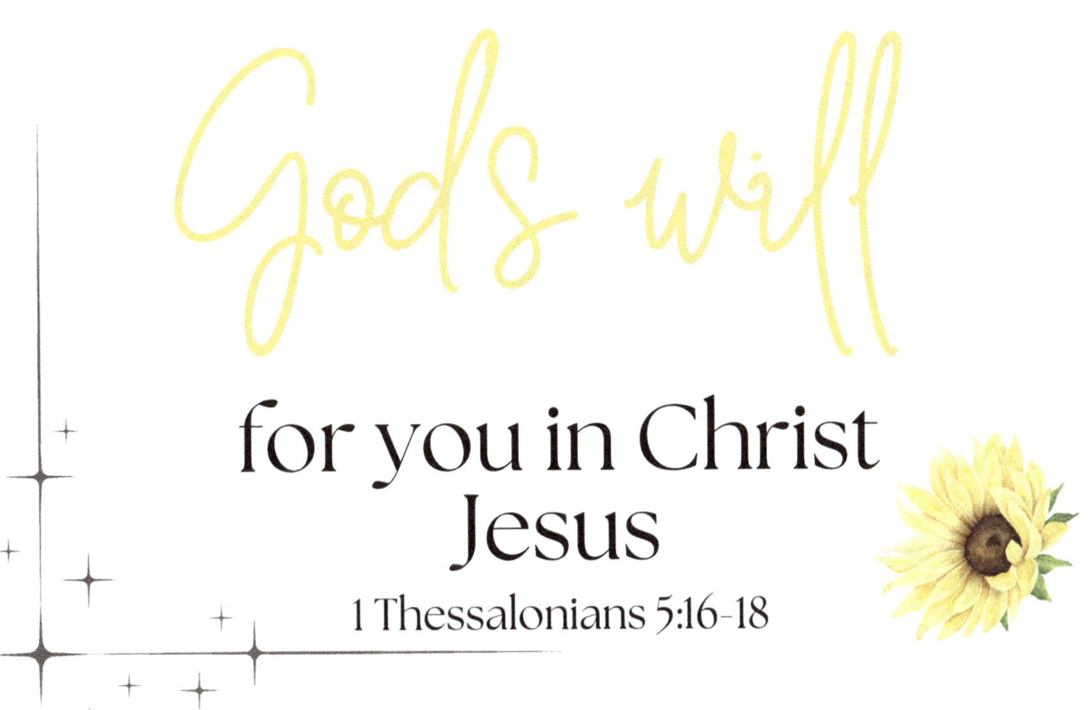

God's will
for you in Christ
Jesus
1 Thessalonians 5:16-18

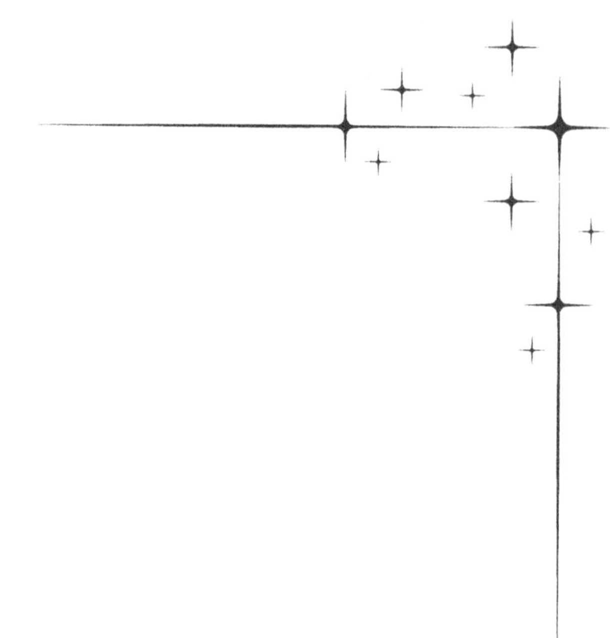
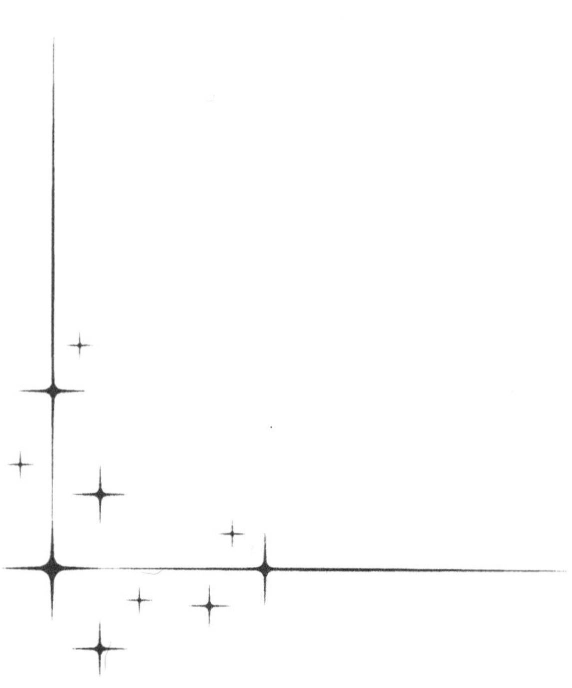

Date: ../../....

Adoration

- ....
- ....
- ....
- ....

Confession

- ....
- ....
- ....
- ....

Thanksgiving

- ....
- ....
- ....
- ....

Supplication

- ....
- ....
- ....
- ....

Today's Scripture

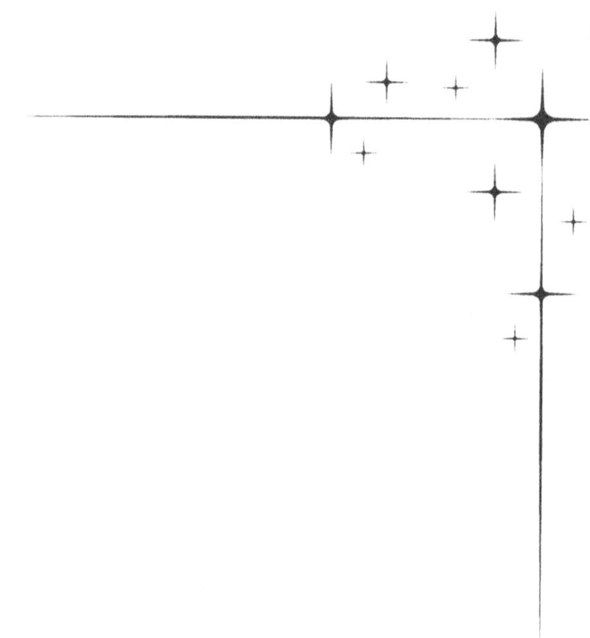
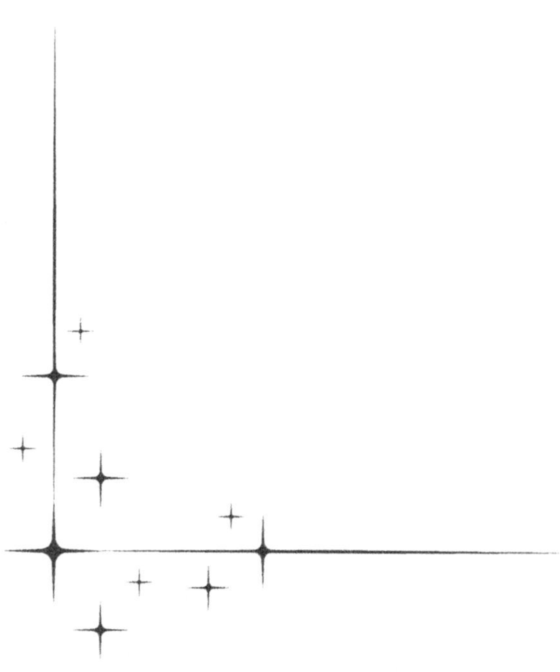

Date: ../../....

Adoration

- ....
- ....
- ....
- ....

Confession

- ....
- ....
- ....
- ....

Thanksgiving

- ....
- ....
- ....
- ....

Supplication

- ....
- ....
- ....
- ....

Today's Scripture

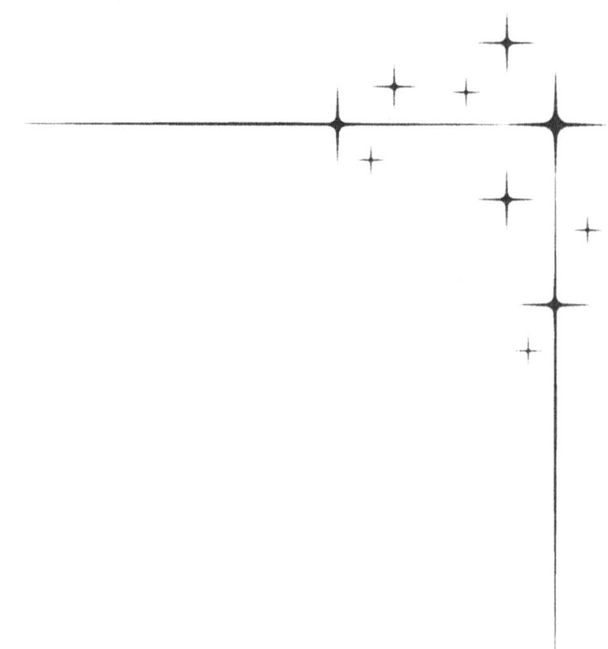
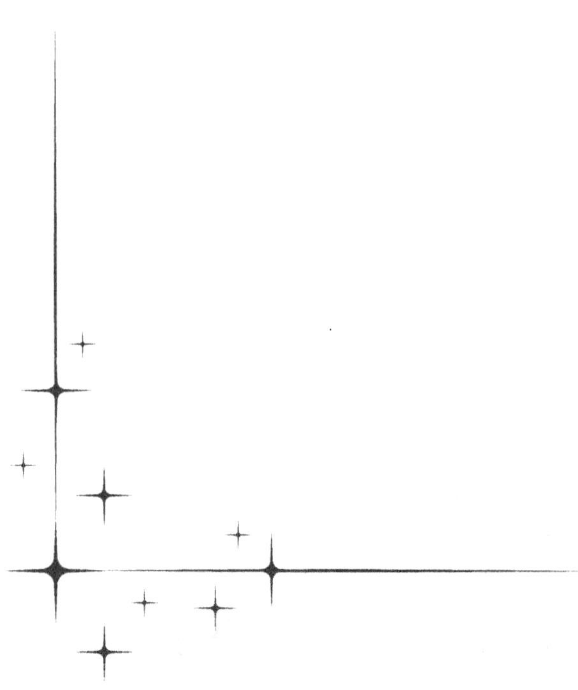

Date: ../../....

Adoration

- ....
- ....
- ....
- ....

Confession

- ....
- ....
- ....
- ....

Thanksgiving

- ....
- ....
- ....
- ....

Supplication

- ....
- ....
- ....
- ....

Today's Scripture

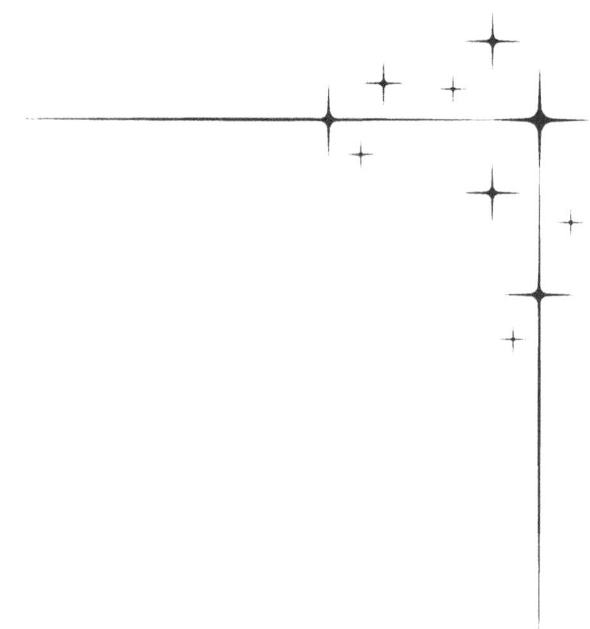
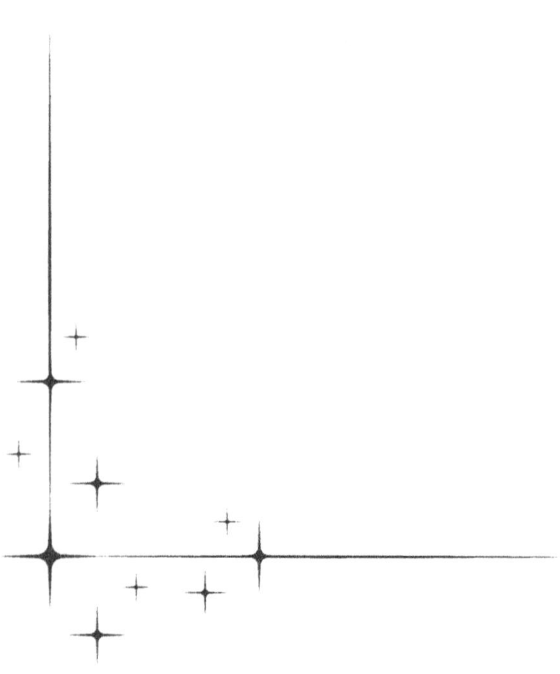

Date: ../../....

Adoration

- ....
- ....
- ....
- ....

Confession

- ....
- ....
- ....
- ....

Thanksgiving

- ....
- ....
- ....
- ....

Supplication

- ....
- ....
- ....
- ....

Today's Scripture

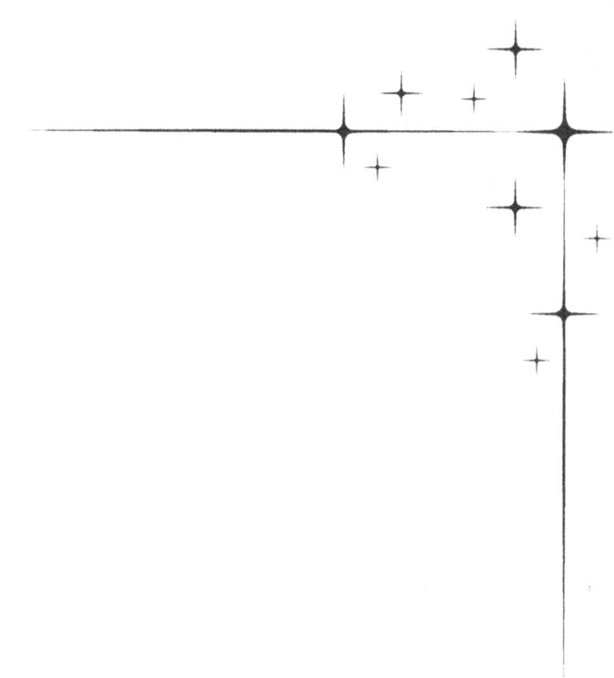
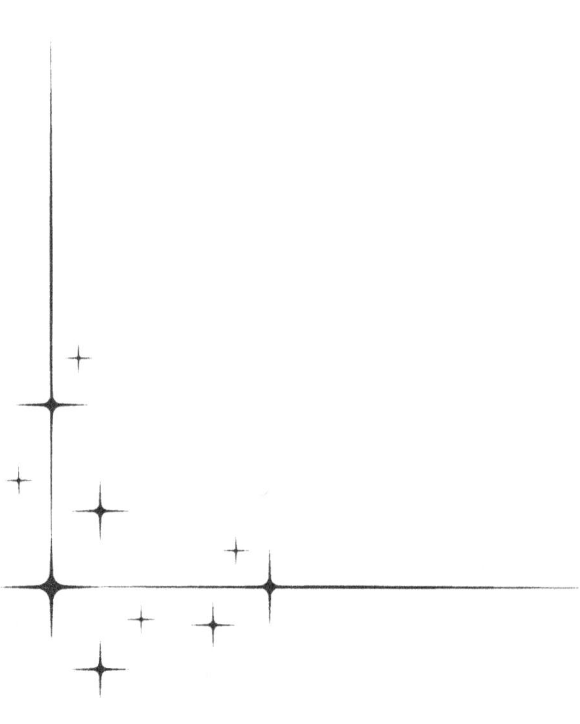

Date: ../../....

Adoration

- ....
- ....
- ....
- ....

Confession

- ....
- ....
- ....
- ....

Thanksgiving

- ....
- ....
- ....
- ....

Supplication

- ....
- ....
- ....
- ....

Today's Scripture

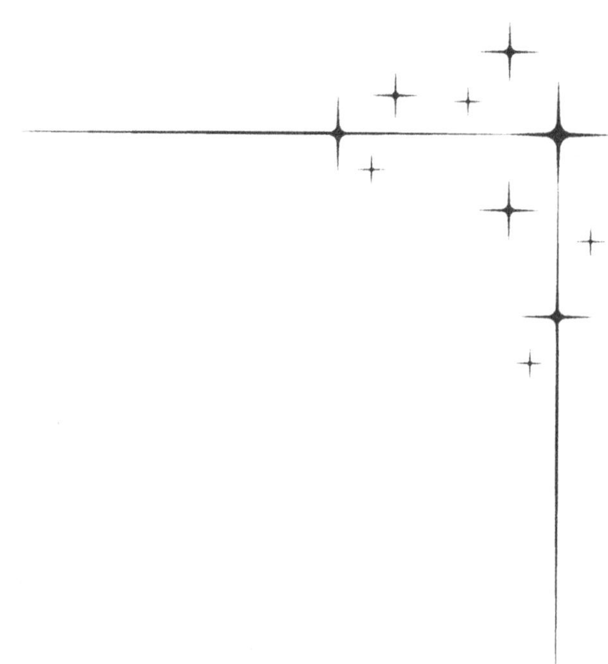
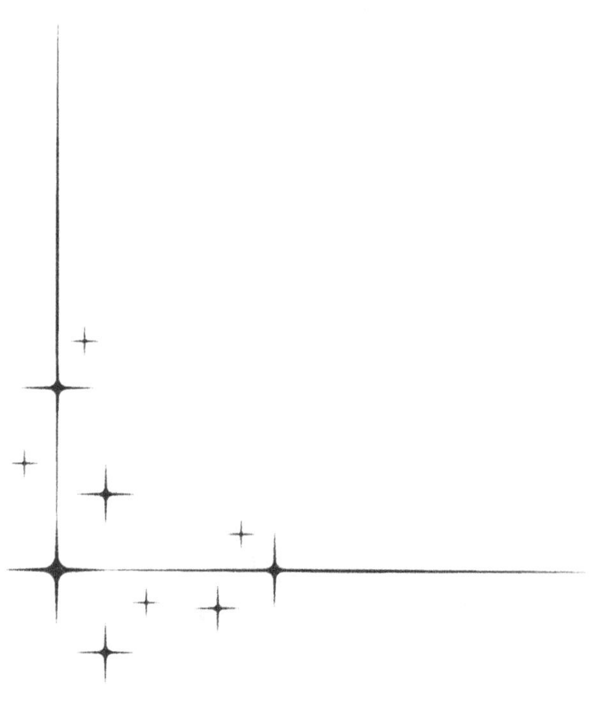

Date: ../../....

Adoration

- ....
- ....
- ....
- ....

Confession

- ....
- ....
- ....
- ....

Thanksgiving

- ....
- ....
- ....
- ....

Supplication

- ....
- ....
- ....
- ....

Today's Scripture

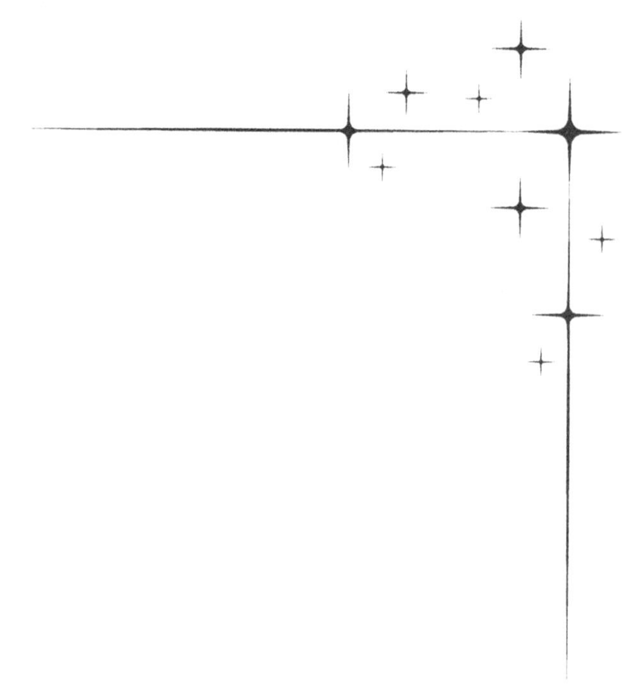
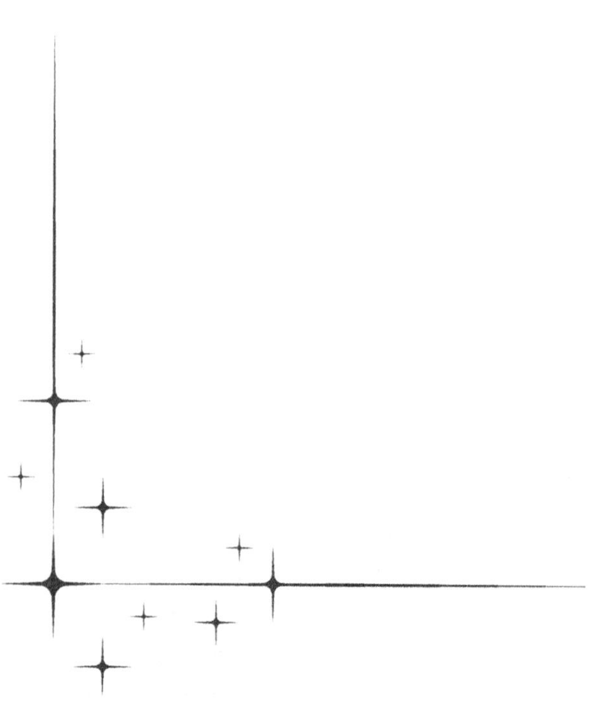

Adoration

- ....
- ....
- ....
- ....

Confession

- ....
- ....
- ....
- ....

Thanksgiving

- ....
- ....
- ....
- ....

Supplication

- ....
- ....
- ....
- ....

Today's Scripture

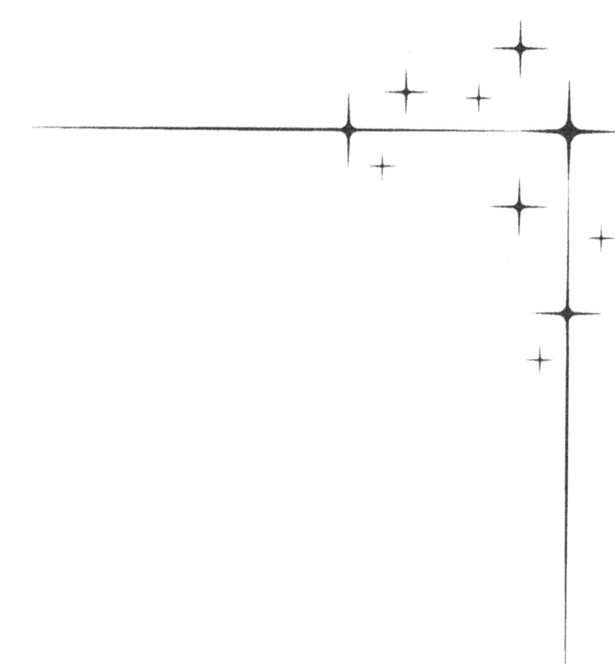
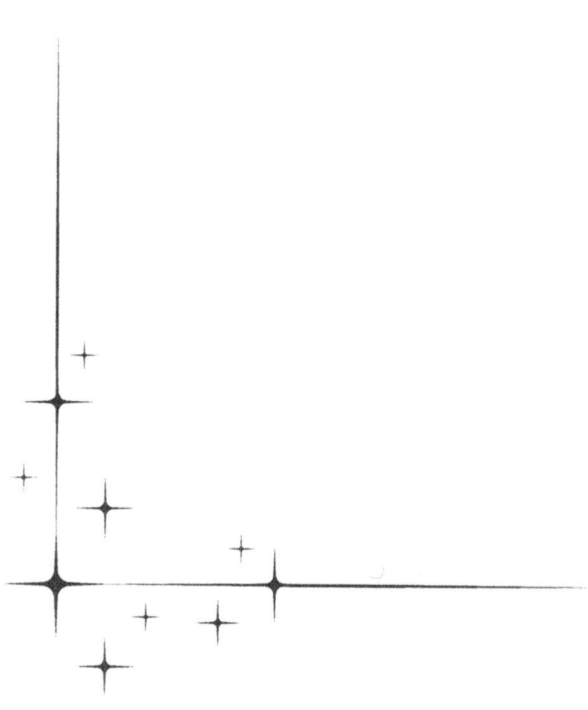

Date: ../../....

Adoration

- ....
- ....
- ....
- ....

Confession

- ....
- ....
- ....
- ....

Thanksgiving

- ....
- ....
- ....
- ....

Supplication

- ....
- ....
- ....
- ....

Today's Scripture

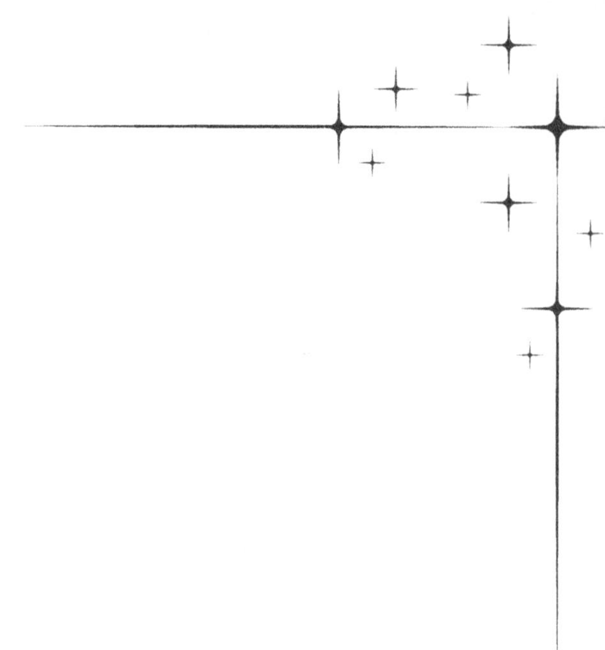
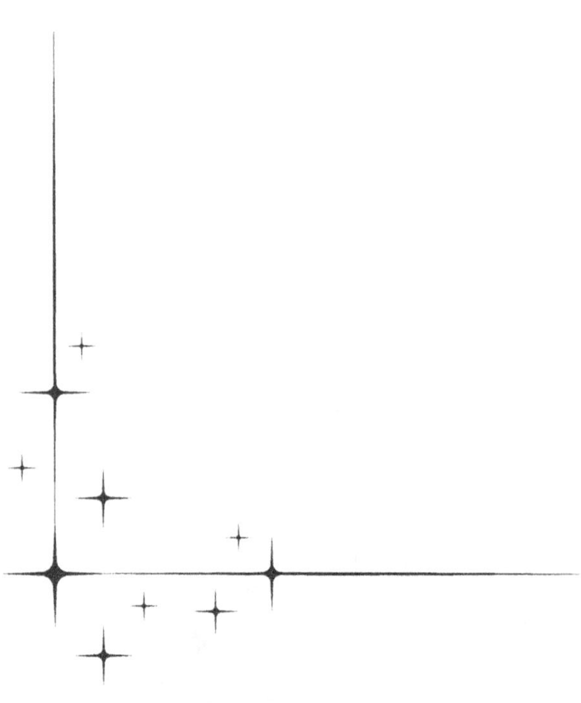

Date: ../../....

Adoration

- ....
- ....
- ....
- ....

Confession

- ....
- ....
- ....
- ....

Thanksgiving

- ....
- ....
- ....
- ....

Supplication

- ....
- ....
- ....
- ....

Today's Scripture

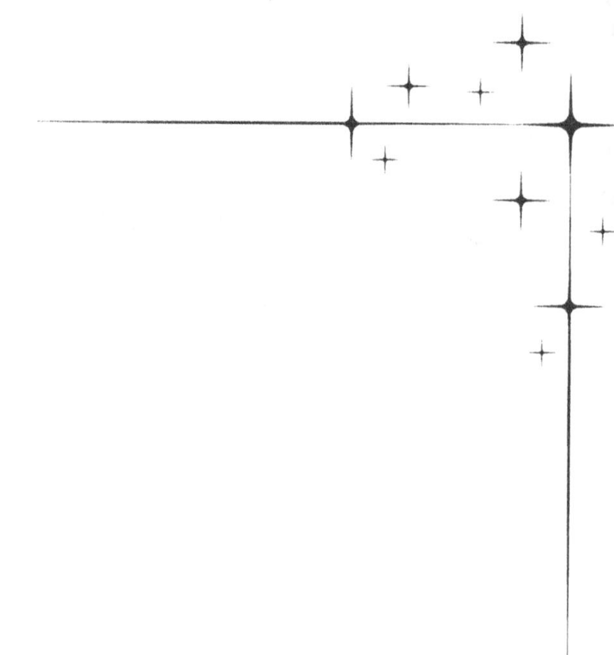
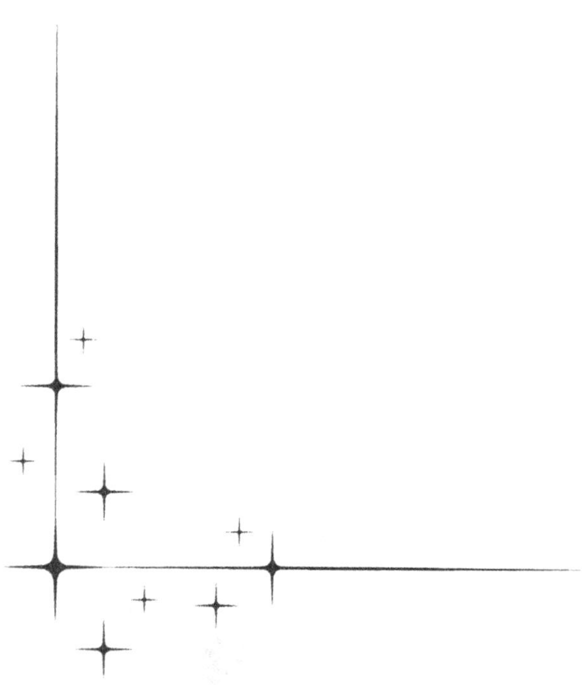

Date: ../../....

Adoration

- ....
- ....
- ....
- ....

Confession

- ....
- ....
- ....
- ....

Thanksgiving

- ....
- ....
- ....
- ....

Supplication

- ....
- ....
- ....
- ....

Today's Scripture

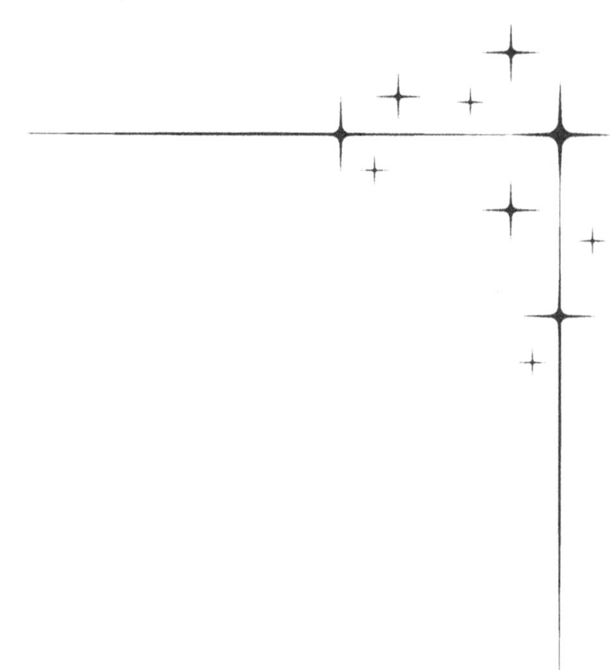
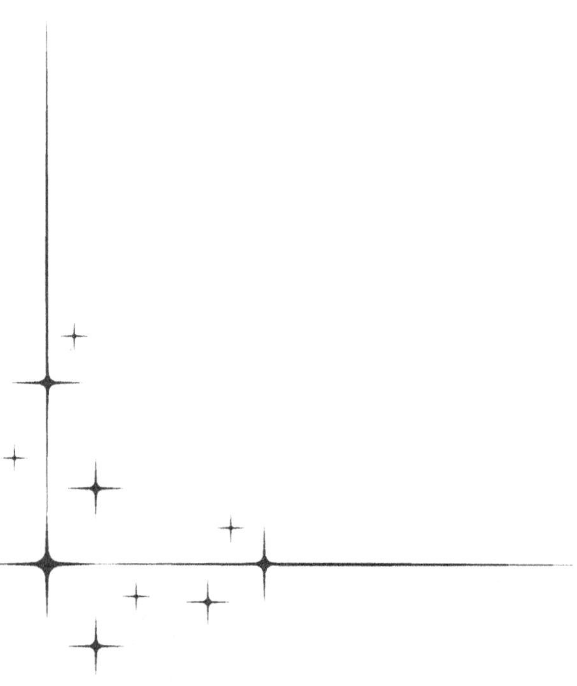

Date: ../../....

Adoration

- ....
- ....
- ....
- ....

Confession

- ....
- ....
- ....
- ....

Thanksgiving

- ....
- ....
- ....
- ....

Supplication

- ....
- ....
- ....
- ....

Today's Scripture

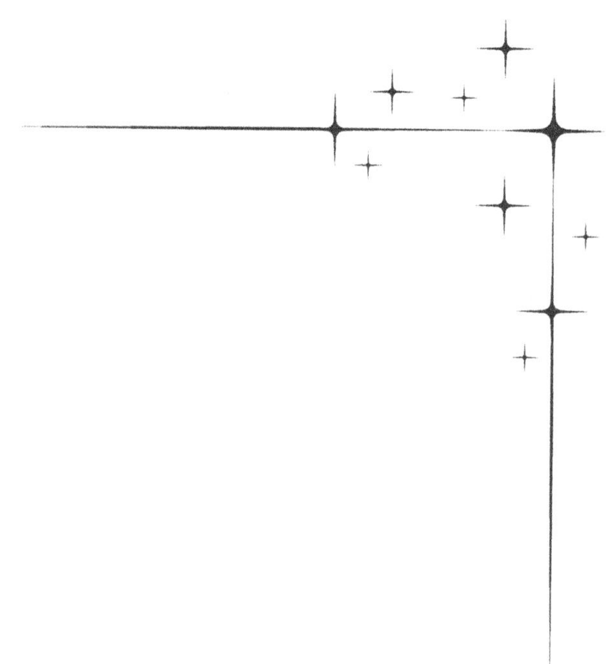
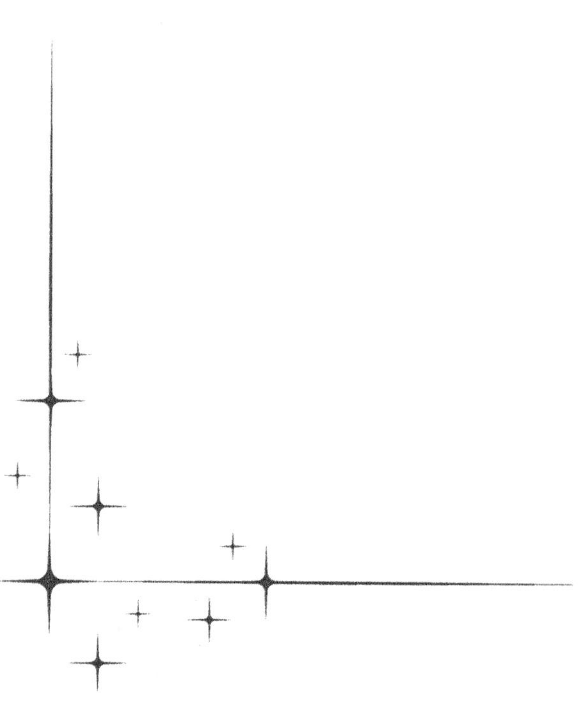

Adoration

- ....
- ....
- ....
- ....

Confession

- ....
- ....
- ....
- ....

Thanksgiving

- ....
- ....
- ....
- ....

Supplication

- ....
- ....
- ....
- ....

Today's Scripture

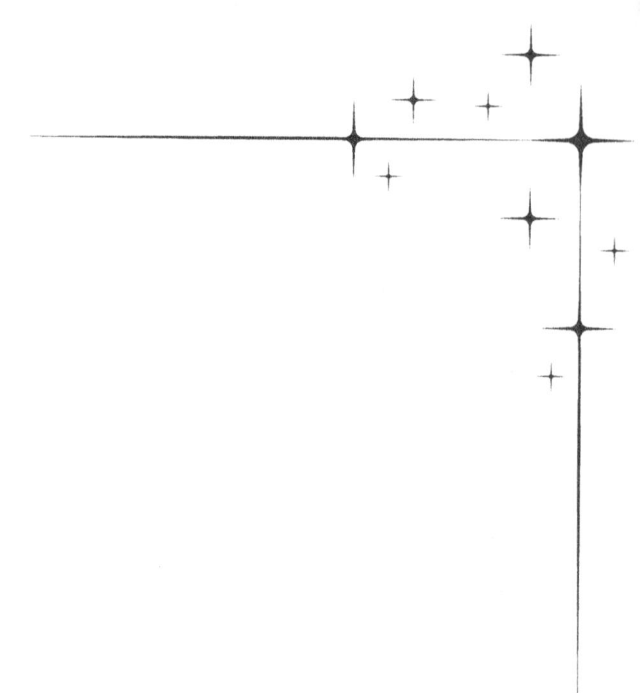
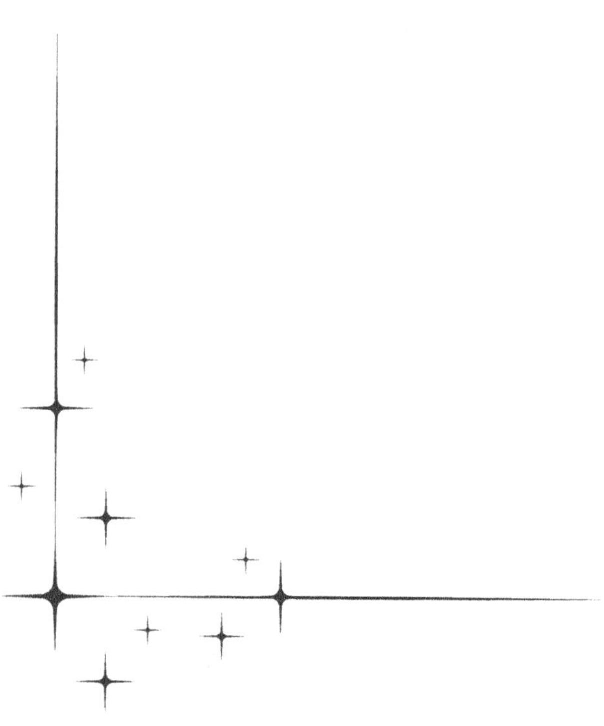

Date: ../../....

Adoration

- ....
- ....
- ....
- ....

Confession

- ....
- ....
- ....
- ....

Thanksgiving

- ....
- ....
- ....
- ....

Supplication

- ....
- ....
- ....
- ....

Today's Scripture

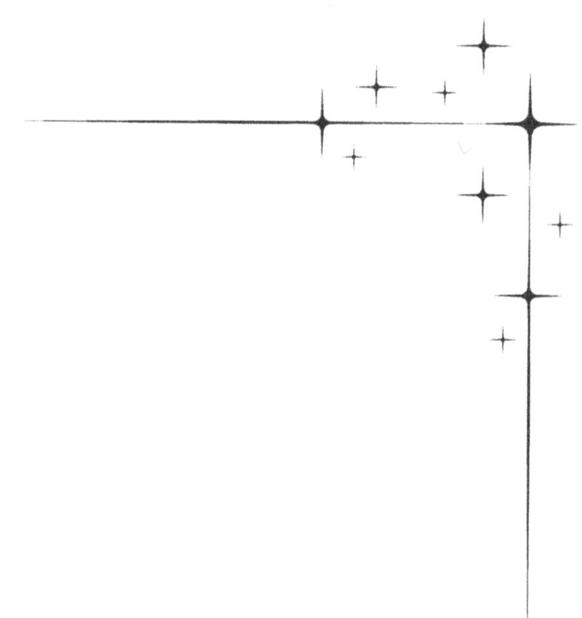
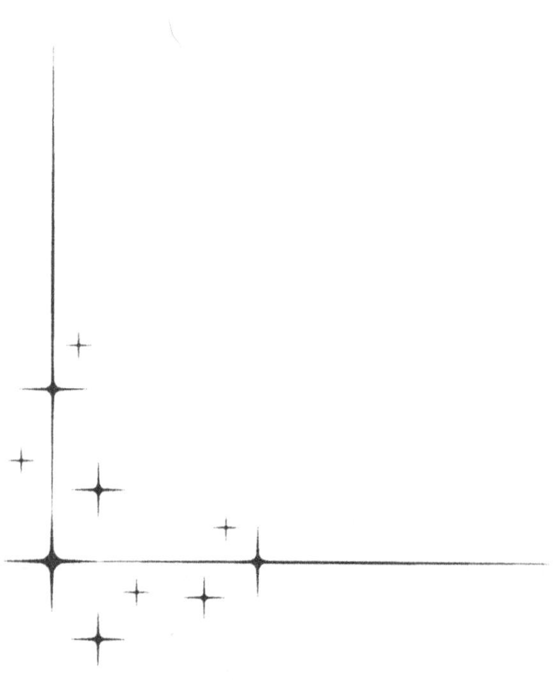

Adoration

- ....
- ....
- ....
- ....

Confession

- ....
- ....
- ....
- ....

Thanksgiving

- ....
- ....
- ....
- ....

Supplication

- ....
- ....
- ....
- ....

Today's Scripture

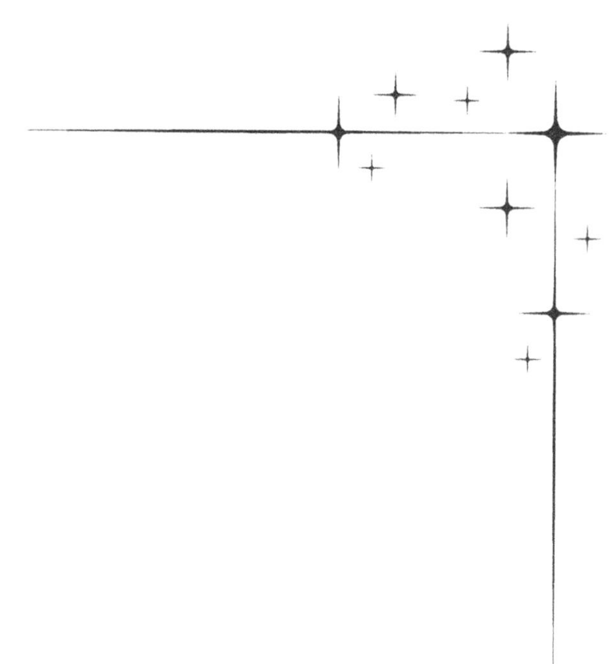
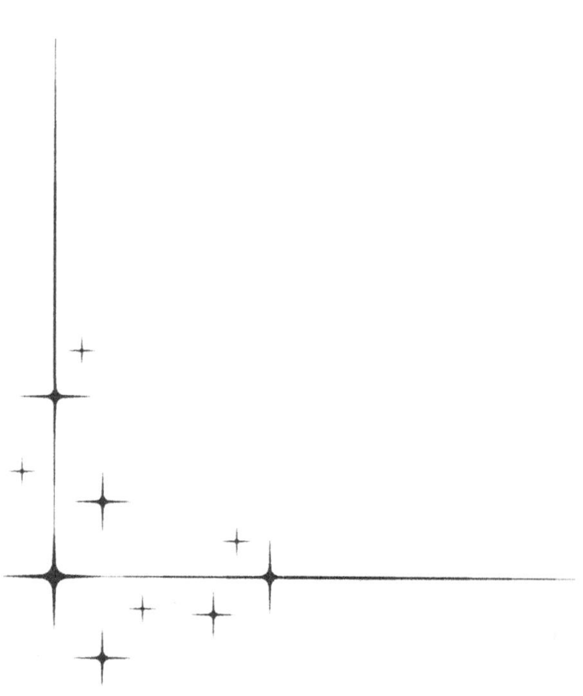

Date: ../../....

Adoration

- ....
- ....
- ....
- ....

Confession

- ....
- ....
- ....
- ....

Thanksgiving

- ....
- ....
- ....
- ....

Supplication

- ....
- ....
- ....
- ....

Today's Scripture

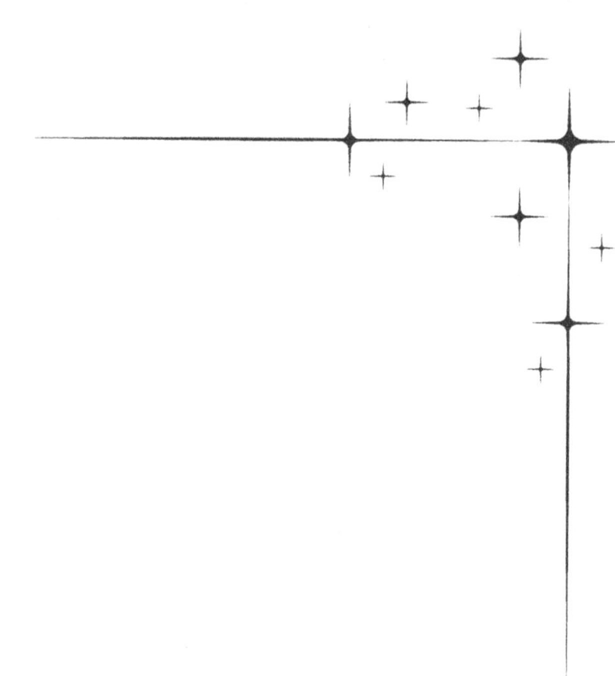

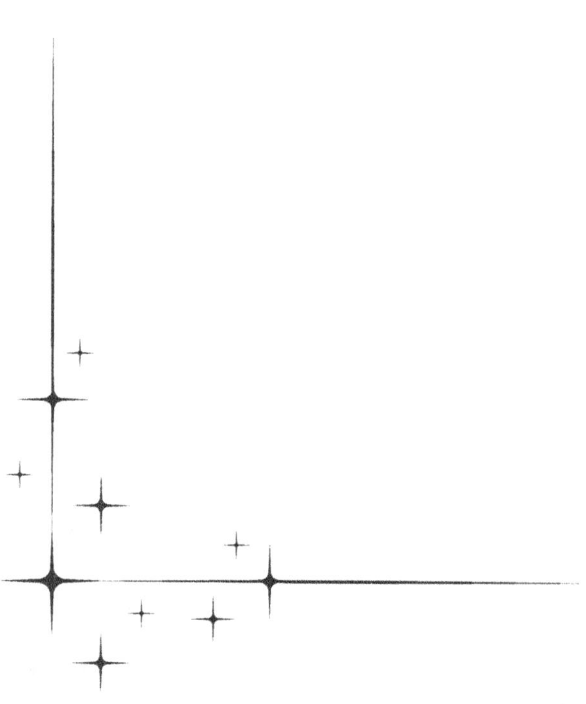

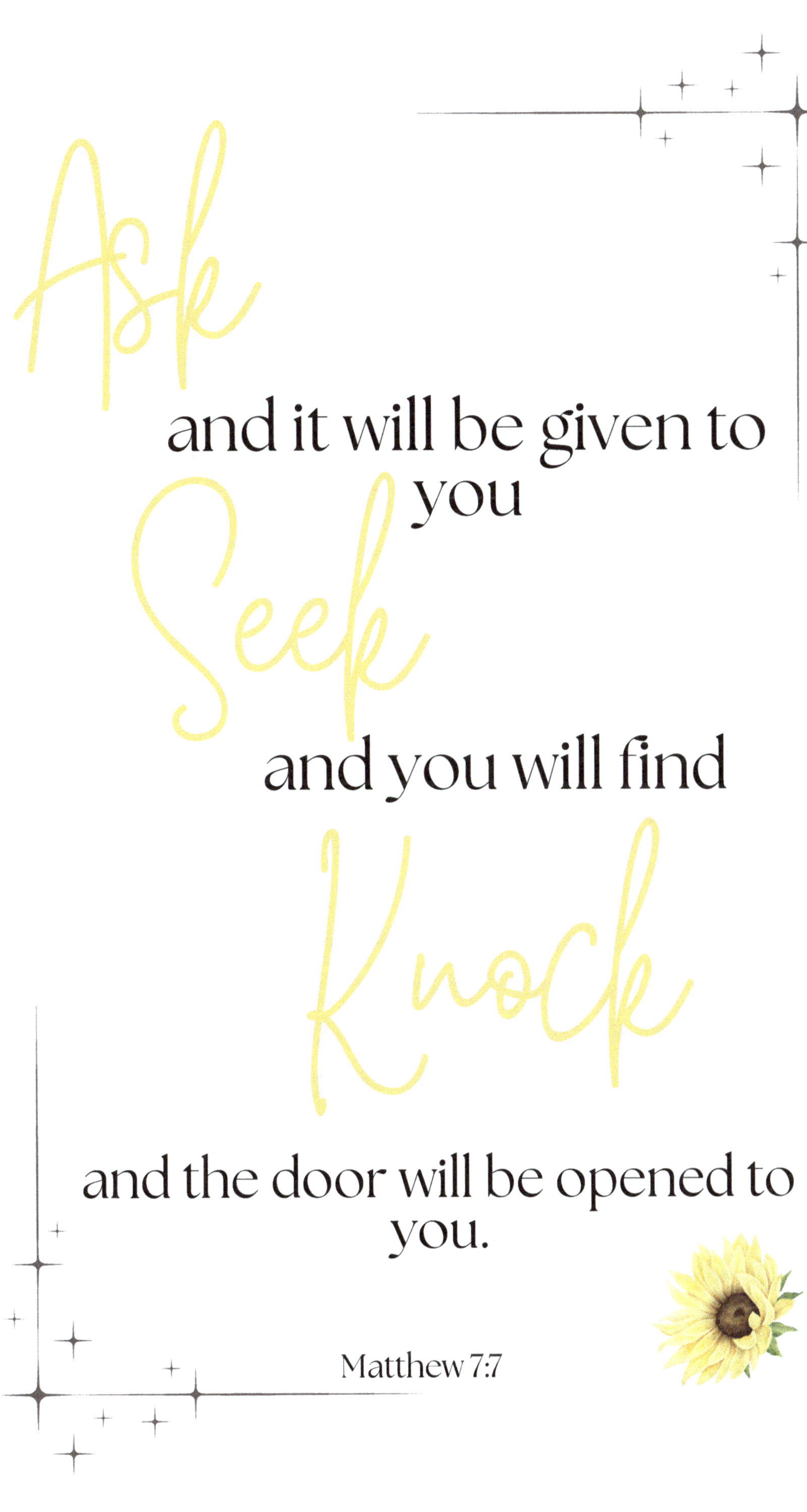

Ask
and it will be given to you
Seek
and you will find
Knock
and the door will be opened to you.
Matthew 7:7

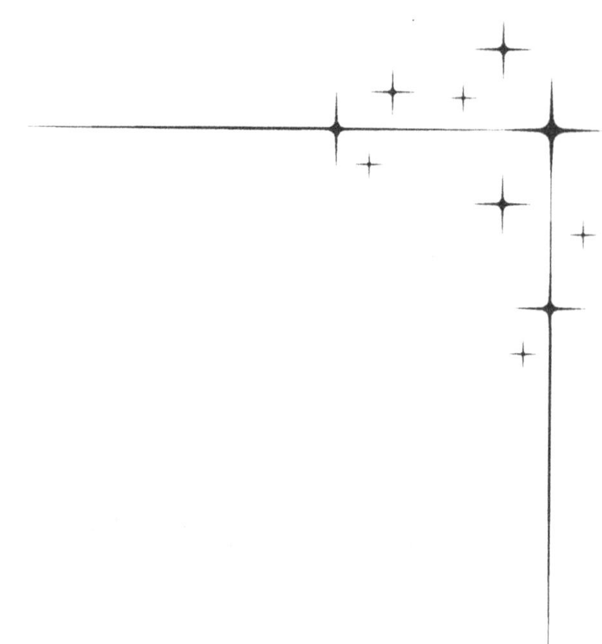
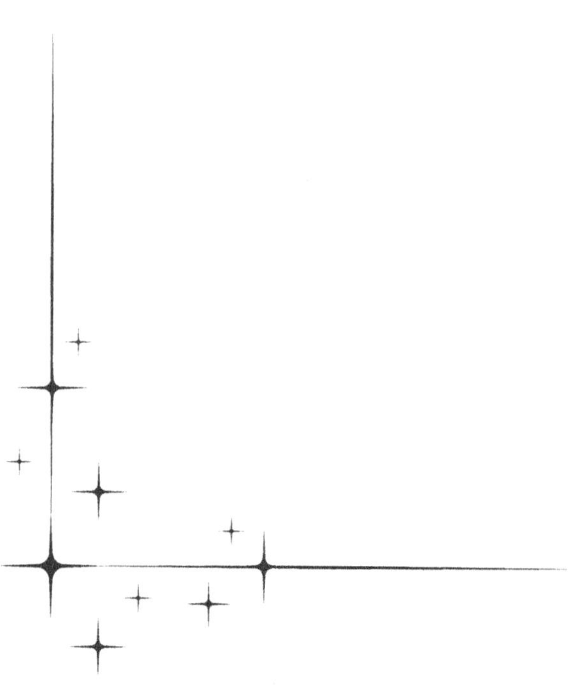

Adoration

- ....
- ....
- ....
- ....

Confession

- ....
- ....
- ....
- ....

Thanksgiving

- ....
- ....
- ....
- ....

Supplication

- ....
- ....
- ....

Today's Scripture

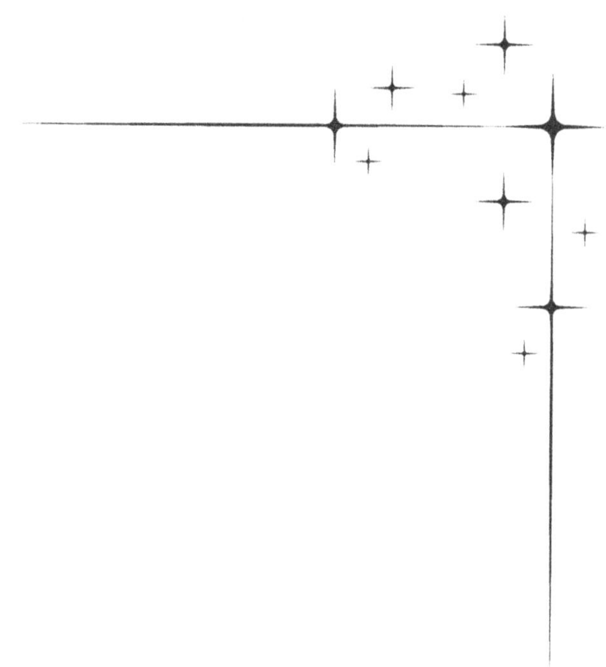
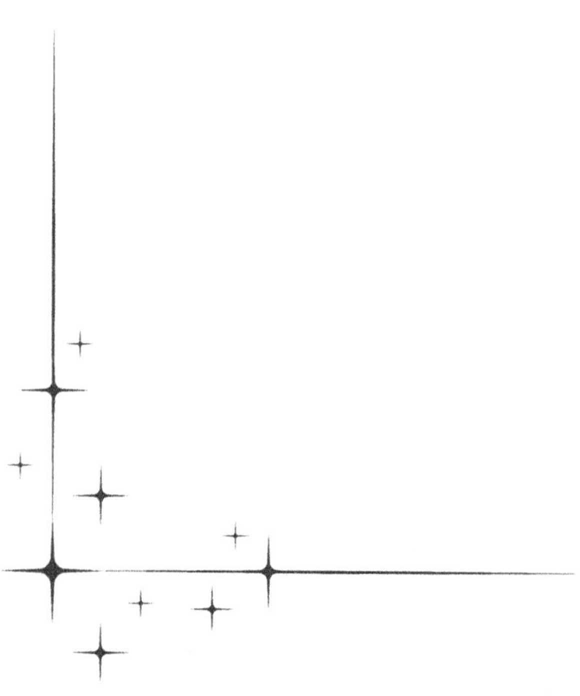

Adoration

- ....
- ....
- ....
- ....

Confession

- ....
- ....
- ....
- ....

Thanksgiving

- ....
- ....
- ....
- ....

Supplication

- ....
- ....
- ....
- ....

Today's Scripture

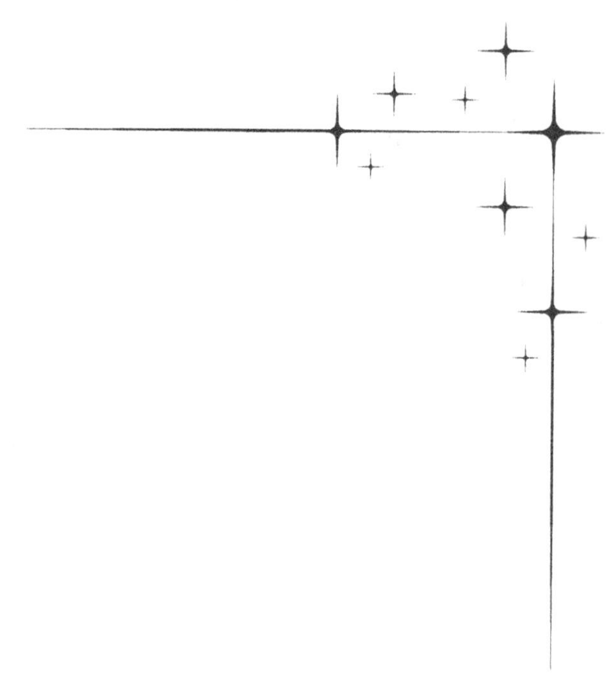
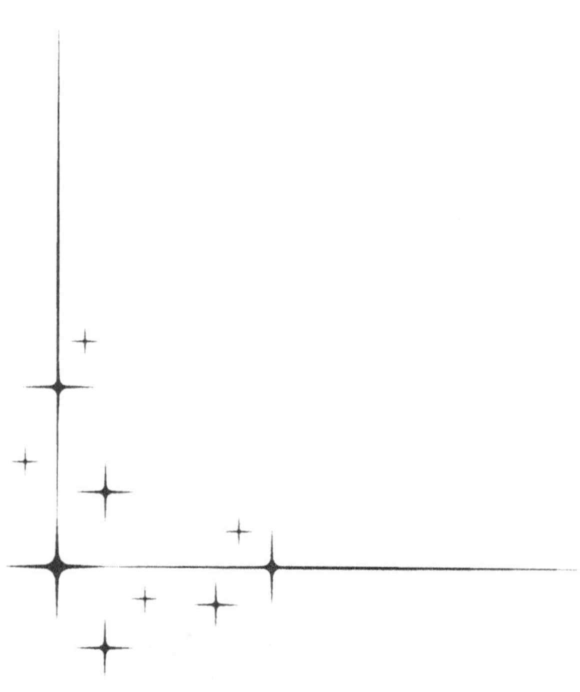

Date: ../../....

Adoration

- ....
- ....
- ....
- ....

Confession

- ....
- ....
- ....
- ....

Thanksgiving

- ....
- ....
- ....
- ....

Supplication

- ....
- ....
- ....
- ....

Today's Scripture

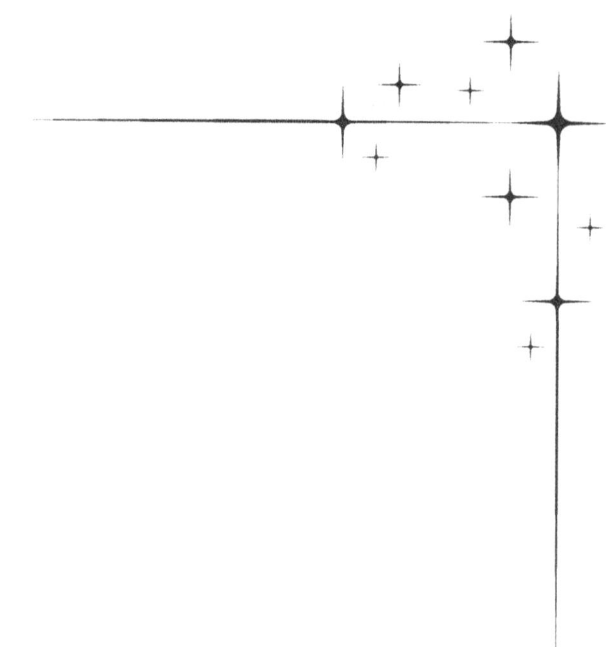
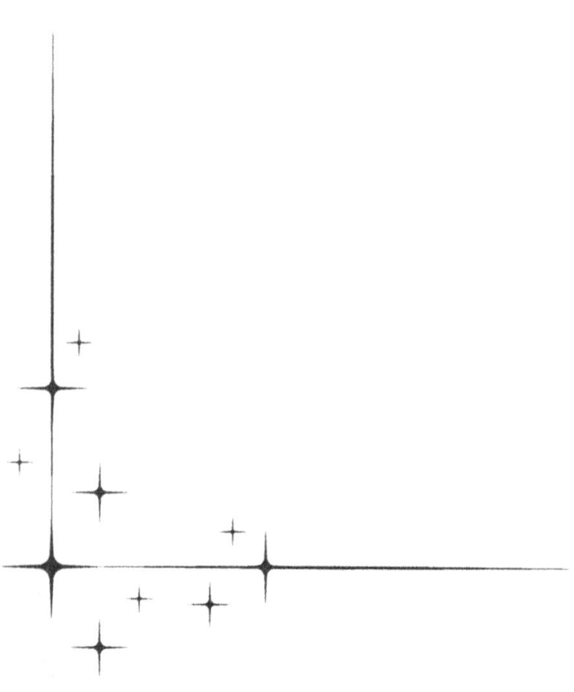

Date: ../../....

Adoration

- ....
- ....
- ....
- ....

Confession

- ....
- ....
- ....
- ....

Thanksgiving

- ....
- ....
- ....
- ....

Supplication

- ....
- ....
- ....
- ....

Today's Scripture

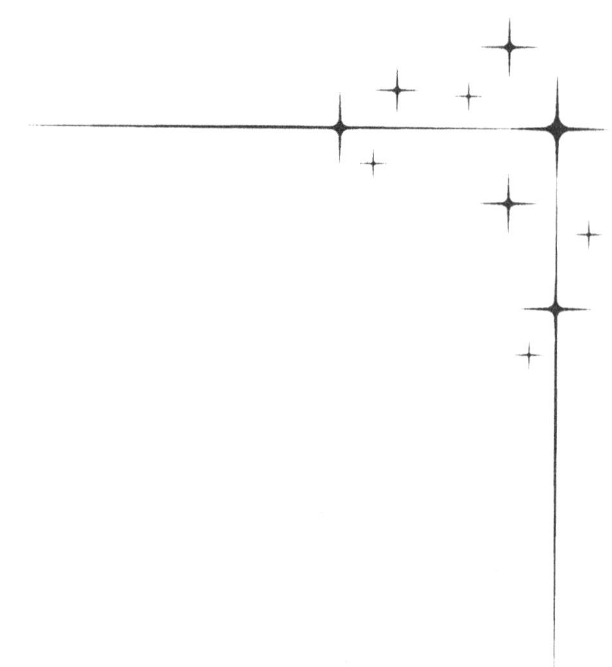
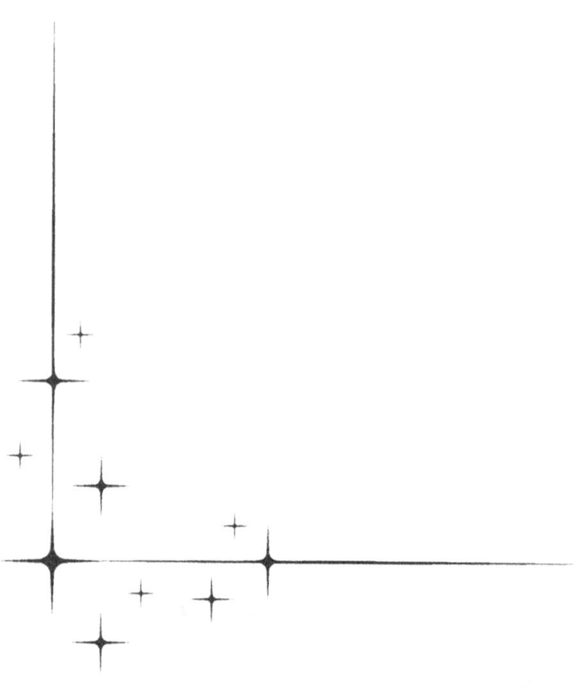

Adoration

- ....
- ....
- ....
- ....

Confession

- ....
- ....
- ....
- ....

Thanksgiving

- ....
- ....
- ....
- ....

Supplication

- ....
- ....
- ....
- ....

Today's Scripture

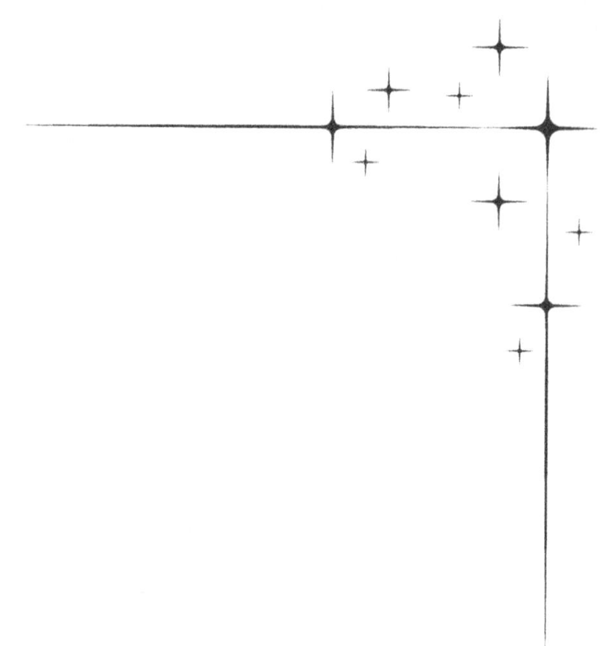
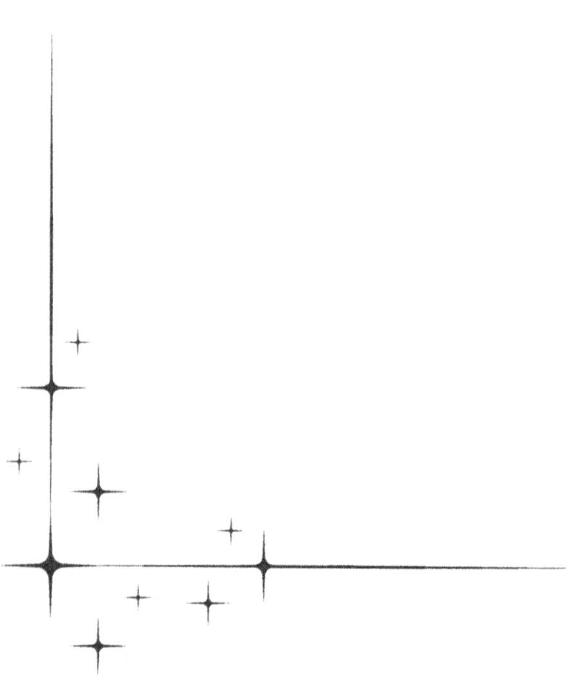

Adoration

- ....

- ....

- ....

- ....

Confession

- ....

- ....

- ....

- ....

Thanksgiving

- ....

- ....

- ....

- ....

Supplication

- ....

- ....

- ....

- ....

Today's Scripture

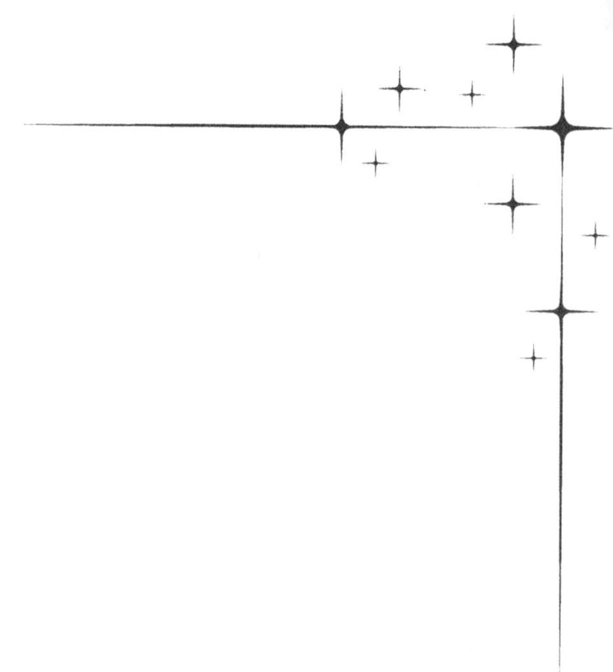

Adoration

- ....
- ....
- ....
- ....

Confession

- ....
- ....
- ....
- ....

Thanksgiving

- ....
- ....
- ....
- ....

Supplication

- ....
- ....
- ....
- ....

Today's Scripture

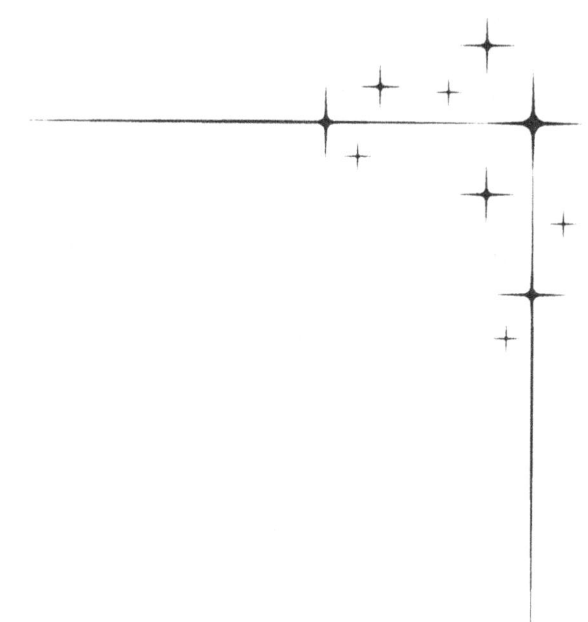
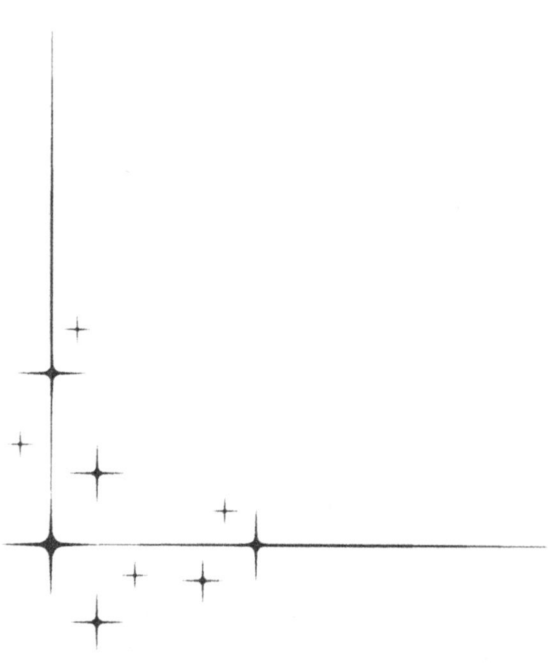

Date: ../../....

Adoration

- ....
- ....
- ....
- ....

Confession

- ....
- ....
- ....
- ....

Thanksgiving

- ....
- ....
- ....
- ....

Supplication

- ....
- ....
- ....
- ....

Today's Scripture

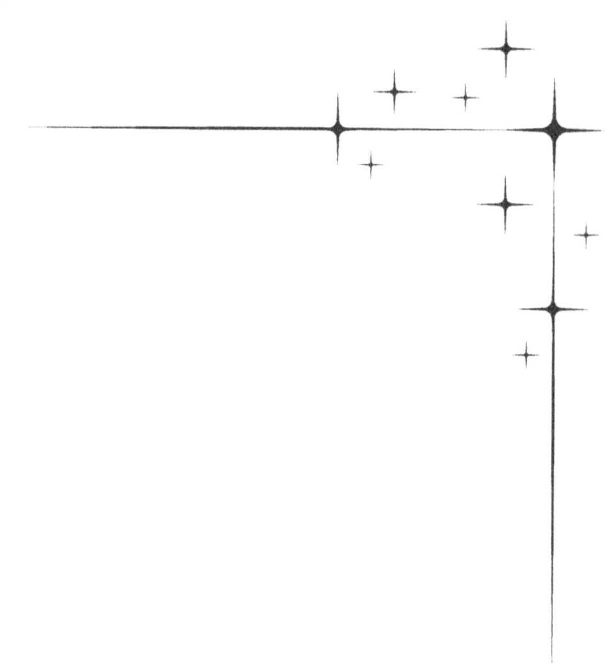
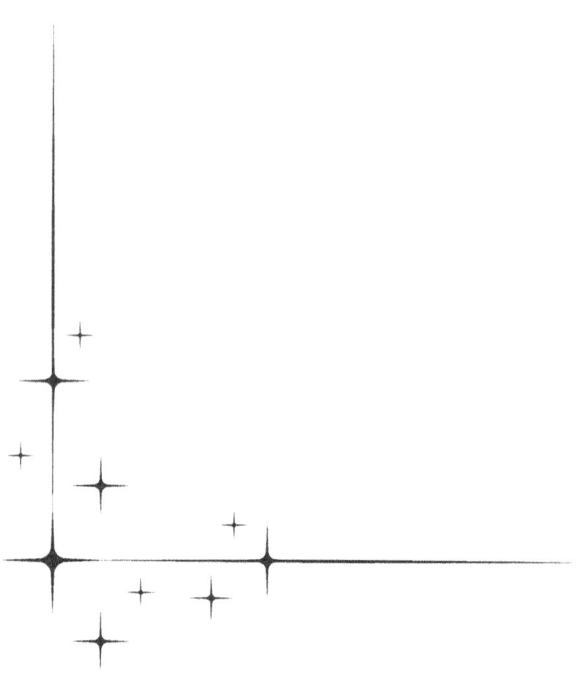

Date: ../../....

Adoration

- ....
- ....
- ....
- ....

Confession

- ....
- ....
- ....
- ....

Thanksgiving

- ....
- ....
- ....
- ....

Supplication

- ....
- ....
- ....
- ....

Today's Scripture

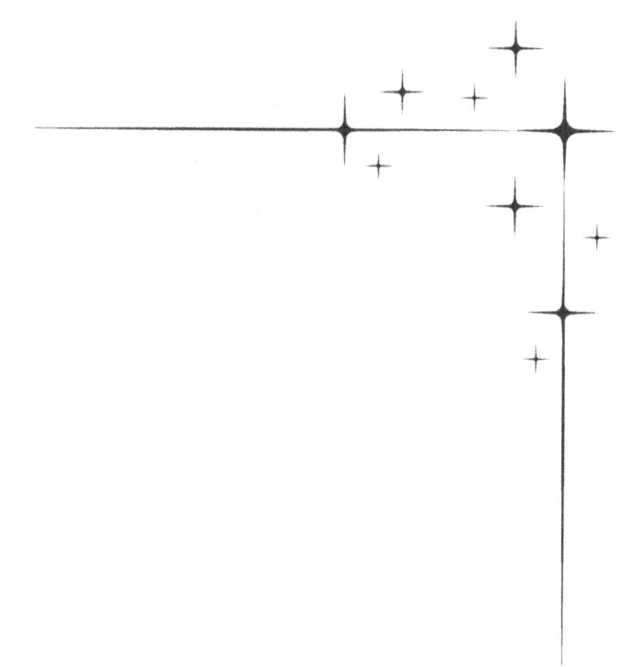
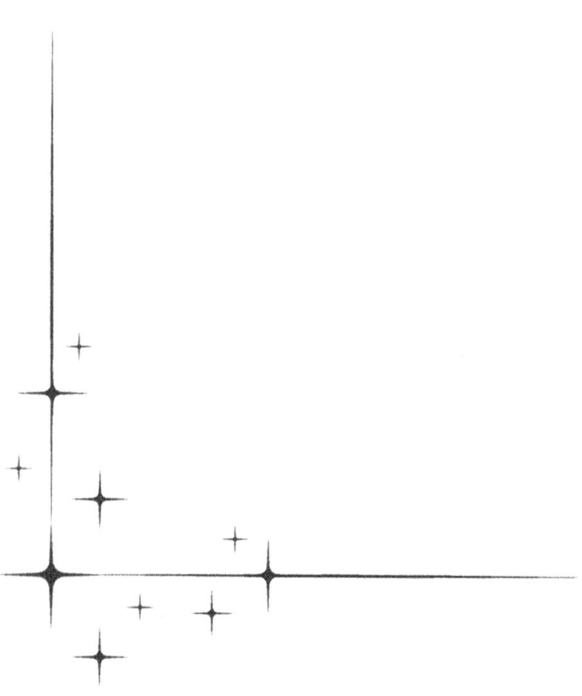

Adoration

- ....
- ....
- ....
- ....

Confession

- ....
- ....
- ....
- ....

Thanksgiving

- ....
- ....
- ....
- ....

Supplication

- ....
- ....
- ....
- ....

Today's Scripture

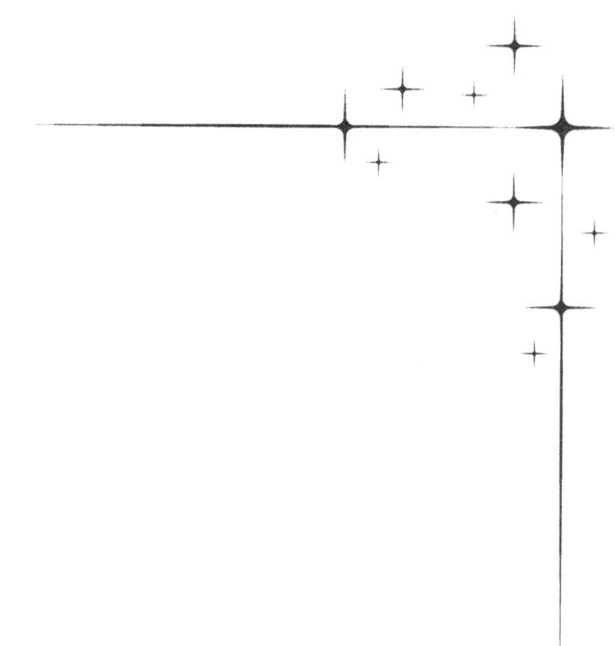
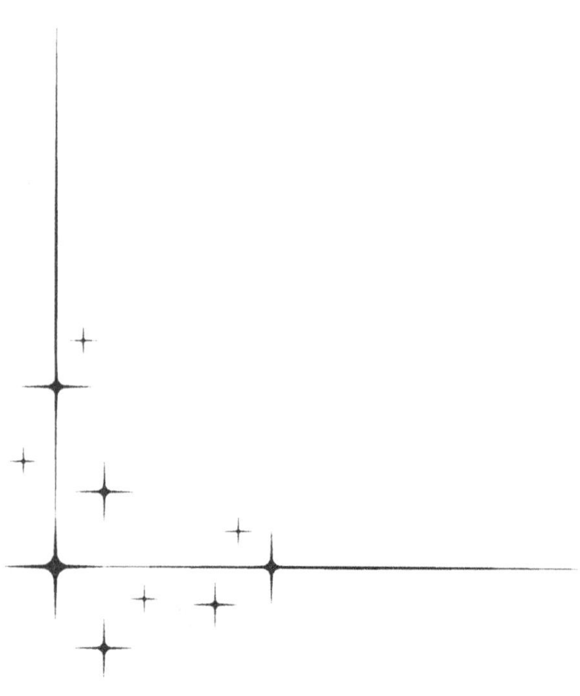

Adoration

- ....
- ....
- ....
- ....

Confession

- ....
- ....
- ....
- ....

Thanksgiving

- ....
- ....
- ....
- ....

Supplication

- ....
- ....
- ....
- ....

Today's Scripture

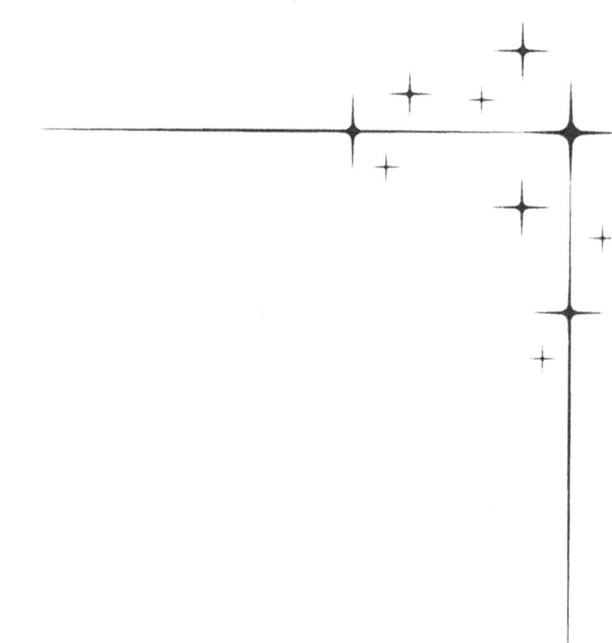
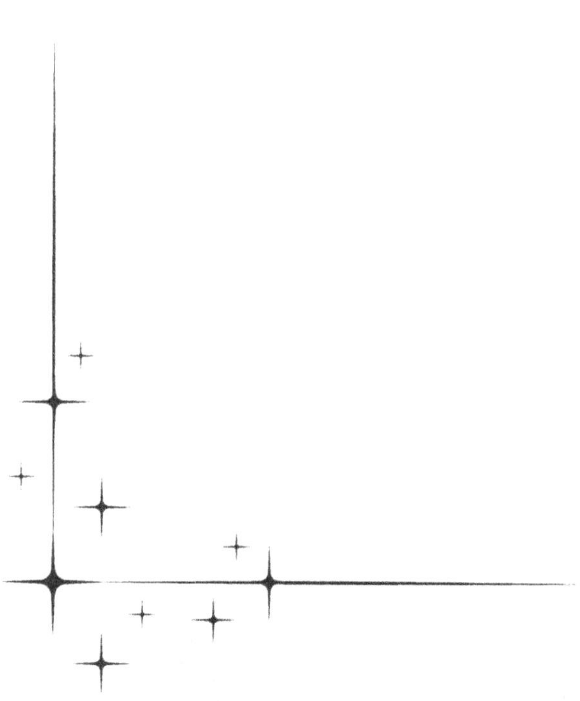

Adoration

- ....
- ....
- ....
- ....

Confession

- ....
- ....
- ....
- ....

Thanksgiving

- ....
- ....
- ....
- ....

Supplication

- ....
- ....
- ....
- ....

Today's Scripture

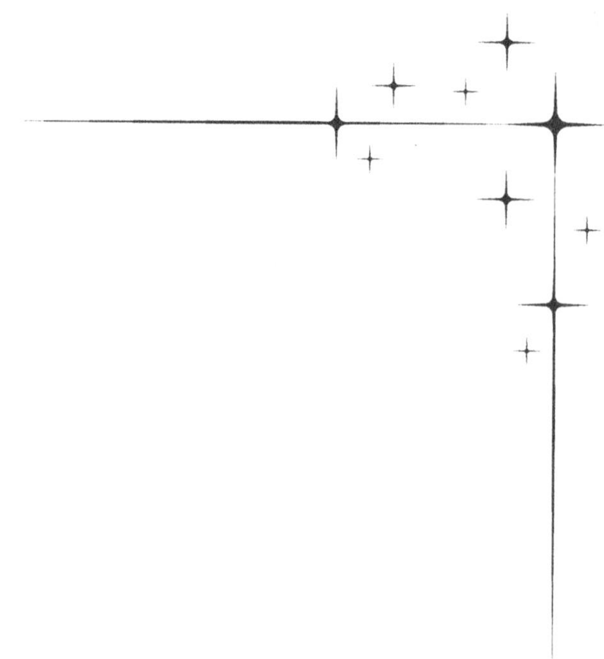
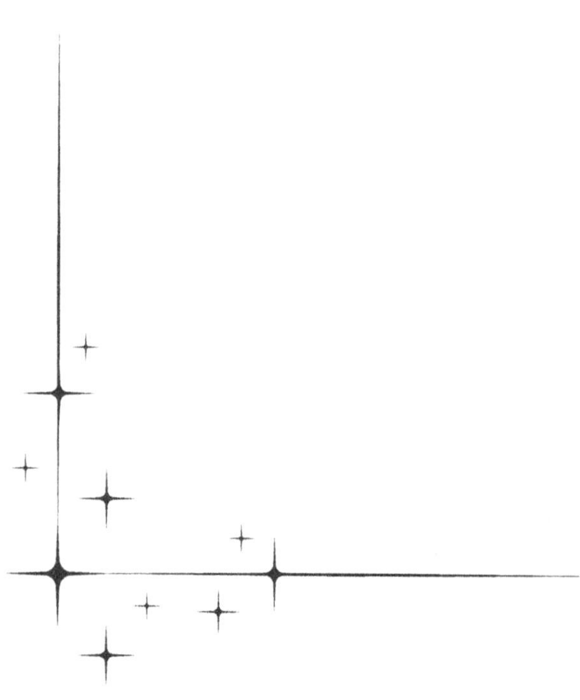

Date: ../../....

Adoration

- ....
- ....
- ....
- ....

Confession

- ....
- ....
- ....
- ....

Thanksgiving

- ....
- ....
- ....
- ....

Supplication

- ....
- ....
- ....
- ....

Today's Scripture

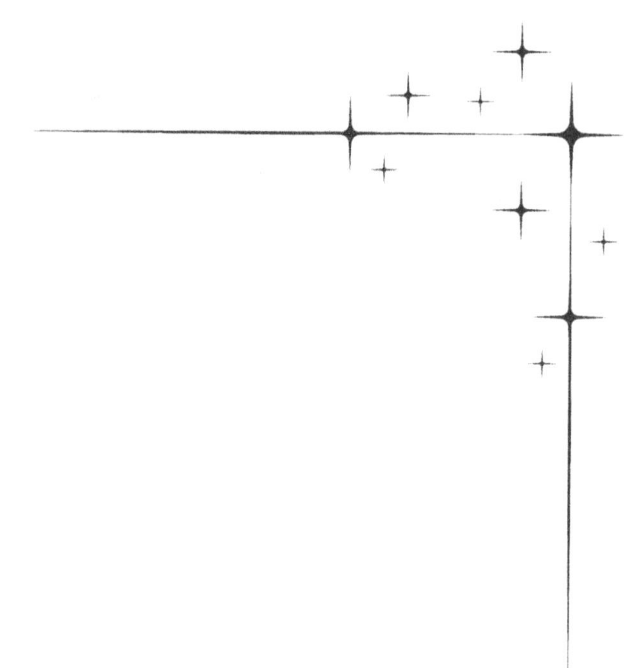
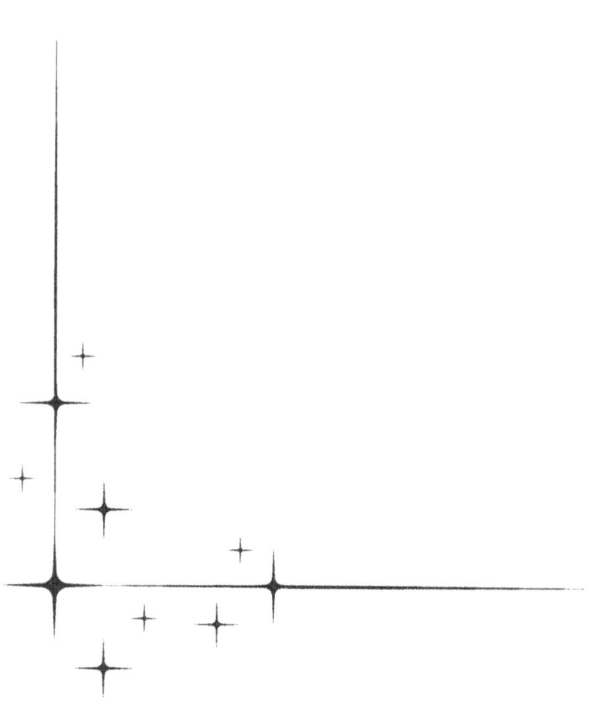

Adoration

- ....
- ....
- ....
- ....

Confession

- ....
- ....
- ....
- ....

Thanksgiving

- ....
- ....
- ....
- ....

Supplication

- ....
- ....
- ....
- ....

Today's Scripture

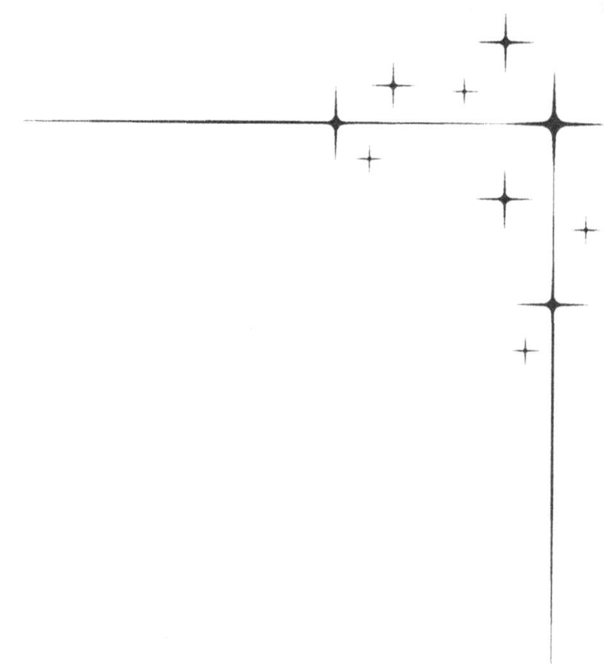
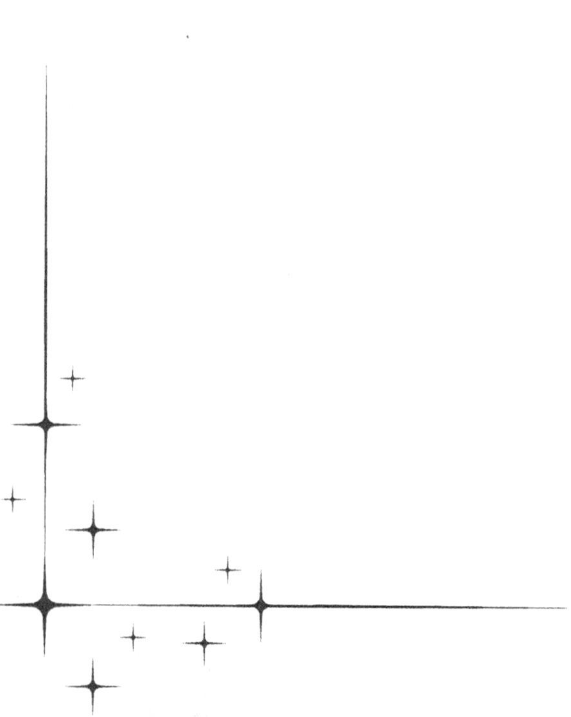

Date: ../../....

Adoration

- ....
- ....
- ....
- ....

Confession

- ....
- ....
- ....
- ....

Thanksgiving

- ....
- ....
- ....
- ....

Supplication

- ....
- ....
- ....
- ....

Today's Scripture

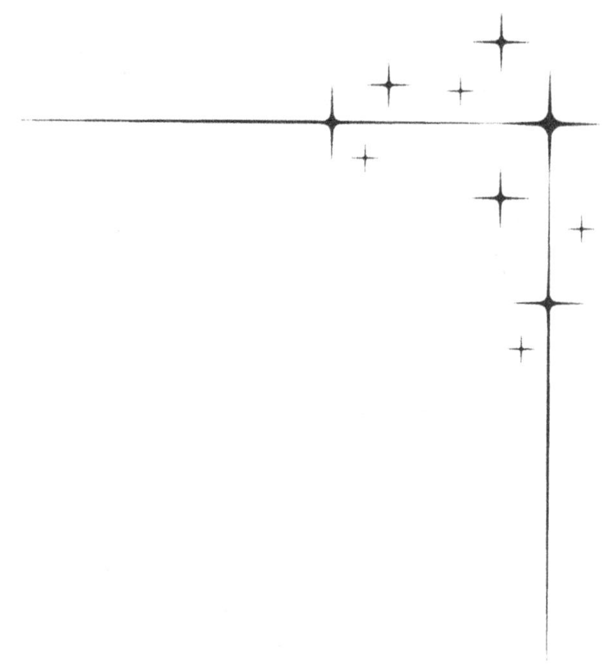
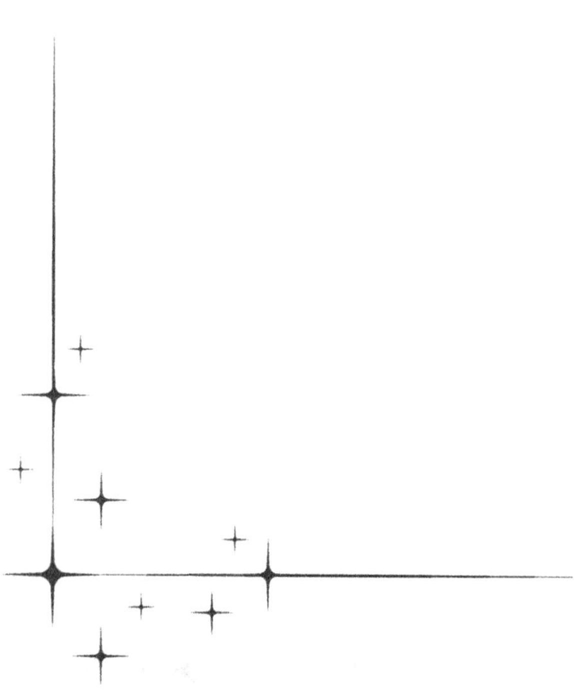

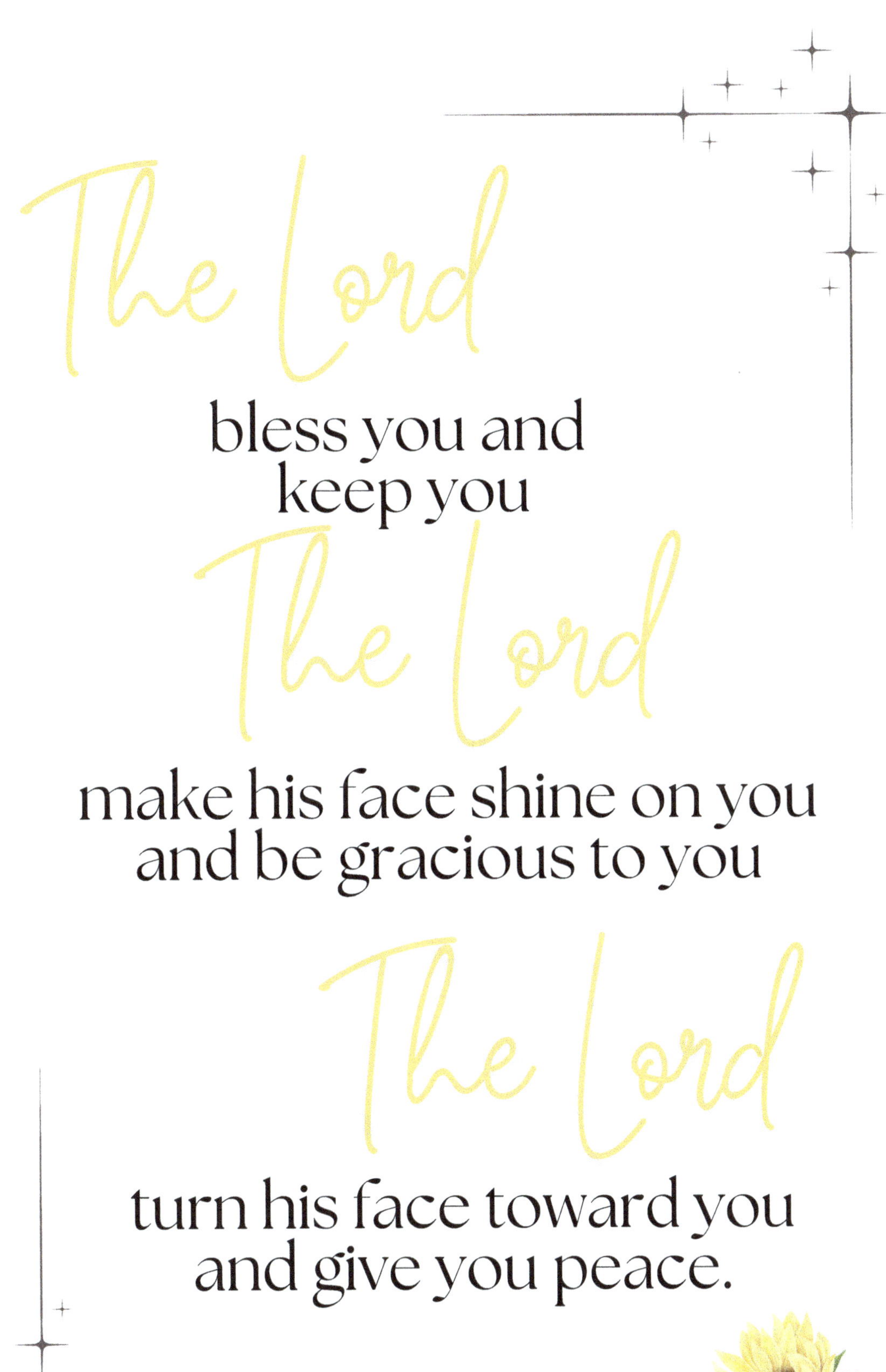

The Lord
bless you and
keep you
The Lord
make his face shine on you
and be gracious to you
The Lord
turn his face toward you
and give you peace.
Numbers 6:24-26